JACK BRICKHOUSE

A VOICE FOR ALL SEASONS

Janice A. Petterchak

FOREWORD BY JEROME HOLTZMAN

CB

CONTEMPORARY BOOKS

A TRIBUNE NEW MEDIA/EDUCATION COMPANY

Library of Congress Cataloging-in-Publication Data

Petterchak, Janice A.
　　Jack Brickhouse : a voice for all seasons / Janice A.
　Petterchak.
　　　　p.　cm.
　　Includes bibliographical references and index.
　　ISBN 0-8092-3207-3
　　1. Brickhouse, Jack, 1916–　　.　2. Sportscasters—United
　States—Biography.　I. Title.
　GV742.42.B75P48　　1996
　070.4'49796'092—dc20
　[B]　　　　　　　　　　　　　　　　　　　　　95-43566
　　　　　　　　　　　　　　　　　　　　　　　　CIP

Grateful acknowledgment is made for permission to use material from the following:

All My Octobers by Mickey Mantle with Mickey Herskowitz
(© 1994, HarperCollins Publishers).

The Bulls and Chicago: A Stormy Affair, courtesy of Bob Logan, *Daily Herald* sportswriter-columnist.

Chicago Tribune, courtesy of the *Chicago Tribune*.

"Jack Brickhouse Reports," courtesy of WGN-TV.

Sox: From Lane and Fain to Zisk and Fisk by Bob Vanderberg, courtesy of Chicago Review Press, Inc.

The Sporting News, courtesy of *The Sporting News*.

Voices of the Game by Curt Smith (© Diamond Communications, Inc, South Bend, IN).

Interior design by Terry Stone

Unless otherwise indicated, all photos are courtesy of Jack Brickhouse.

Published by Contemporary Books, Inc.
Two Prudential Plaza, Chicago, Illinois 60601-6790
Manufactured in the United States of America
International Standard Book Number: 0-8092-3207-3
10　9　8　7　6　5　4　3　2　1

TO EMIL AND VERA
Baseball Fans

Contents

Foreword

ALL OF US SHOULD GIVE THANKS FOR JACK BRICKHOUSE. He has been in our midst for more than a half century, as good a man as can be found in a long day's march. Cheerful almost beyond compare, he ladles praise with a kindly hand. I had assumed he's never met anyone he didn't like.

To my delight, I have discovered the honeymoon ended when he was confronted with Leo Durocher. The Lip managed the Cubs for six and a half years. I didn't like him, either, and gave him a few well-deserved knocks. Characteristically, good-guy Brickhouse held his tongue. But now, 20 years later, he has put on the gloves.

Durocher should have been grateful to him. It was Brickhouse who convinced Philip K. Wrigley, the late Cub caretaker, that he should hire him. But soon after Durocher arrived, he learned that Ernie Banks was "Mr. Cub," and that Brickhouse was the most influential figure in Chicago sports.

"He resented Banks and me," Brickhouse explains. "The way he treated Banks was brutal, one of the cruelest things I've ever seen. Leo hated to share the spotlight, and he took it out on Banks, and some of that jealousy was directed at me."

It is the only paragraph of criticism in Janice Petterchak's wonderfully thorough biography of John Beasley Brickhouse. I have known Brickhouse for 40 years. Prior to this book I thought I knew him fairly well. Now I know him better than ever and am standing up to cheer.

His story is inspirational, the fulfillment of the American dream, a Horatio Alger epic: Born in Peoria, the son of a wandering minstrel, Jack Brickhouse was raised in modest circumstances. His boyhood struggles are well chronicled, as well as his Chicago success. Long before he retired he was among the country's very best sports broadcasters—and he did it without knocking anyone and calling attention to himself.

Brickhouse is from the "gee whiz" school as opposed to the "aw nuts" genre epitomized by the late Howard Cosell. "I've debated Howard about this," Brickhouse has revealed. "I told him he's got his act, I've got mine. . . . All this personal stuff about athletes' lives. . . . I don't want to be a stick-in-the-mud, but when you go overboard, you don't hurt the athlete only. You hurt his wife going to the grocery store, his kid going to school. Why? What does it prove?

"I've done more TV baseball than any broadcaster ever, and I'd be lying if I said that every day, I couldn't wait to get to the ballpark. But whenever I wasn't up, I'd open a letter from some shut-in or look behind home plate at all those people in wheelchairs. If, somehow, I helped provide an escape, then maybe I did a decent job."

Bravo for Brickhouse! He realized he was reporting sports, not the Nuremberg Trials. Because of his fair-minded approach he was on the inside-of-the-inside. But he never told anybody about it. For example, he saved the White Sox for Chicago.

Aware that owner John Allyn was on the edge of bankruptcy and that the American League was insisting Allyn move the club to Seattle, Brickhouse hurried to the rescue and helped save the White Sox for Chicago by helping find investors and supply Bill Veeck with the capital needed to buy the club.

This work is more than a Brickhouse biography. It is a history of the Chicago sports scene, much of it previously untold. More than anyone else in the so-called media, he was the confidant of the owners and the principal executives who operated Chicago's professional sports franchises.

No one was in the booth longer or knew as many ballplayers. His career dates back to the time when J. Louis Comiskey owned the White Sox, Jimmy Dykes was managing, and Luke Appling was the club's star shortstop.

He tells of the incident when Appling was asked by the Red Cross in his Atlanta, Georgia, hometown for autographed baseballs to sell at a war-time fundraiser:

"Luke asked the Sox for a couple dozen baseballs. While he was getting ready for batting practice, he got the word that club vice president Harry Grabiner had turned him down—'Can't spare them.' Luke sent the messenger back to tell Grabiner, 'You'd better come out and watch my batting practice.' Grabiner went and watched as Luke fouled twelve straight pitches into the seats. On the last one Grabiner yelled, 'You've got them. You can have the baseballs.'"

These wonderful anecdotes about both the Cubs and White Sox abound. Brickhouse tells us about Nellie Fox, Billy Pierce, and Early Wynn and how the White Sox won the 1959 pennant, Chicago's last flag; of the ill-fated Lou Brock–Ernie

Broglio trade; the 1969 Cubs of Ernie Banks, Billy Williams, Ron Santo, and Ferguson Jenkins; the day at Wrigley Field, in a game against the St. Louis Cardinals, when two balls were in play; and what happened when White Sox general manager Frank Lane, in an effort to increase home run production, brought in the left-field fence. Instead of helping the Sox, opposing players hit eleven home runs in the first eight games.

"I'm driving Lane home and he's boiling," Brickhouse reveals. "He is just absolutely frying. We're driving up Lake Shore Drive past Oak Street Beach. I said, 'Frank, don't worry about it. Take your mind off it. Take a look at all those beautiful girls out there in their bathing suits. . . .' But in order to see them he had to look through another wire fence. He finally yelled, 'All I can see is that lousy fence!'

"And so now we get home, and about one o'clock in the morning, after he'd been stewing and fretting about it all night long, . . . he got poor Leo Dillon, the maintenance chief, out of bed and whipped that crew out there to that ballpark in the middle of the night, and that fence was down by the time the Yankees came out to the ballpark the next day."

This is sports at its best. And, if you agree, there is much good reading ahead.

Jerome Holtzman
Chicago Tribune

Introduction

To CHICAGO WRITER KENAN HEISE, JACK BRICKHOUSE is a storyteller, "perhaps one in the last generation of genuine storytellers." A narrator of stories from decades past and from yesterday, he is a popular and lively raconteur: whether at informal gatherings or as a featured speaker or panelist, he always has stories. This biography, then, is based on stories, his reminiscences from grammar school through six decades of a broadcasting career, especially his forty years as the voice of baseball's Chicago Cubs and his twenty-five years with the White Sox.

In 1986 Brickhouse published *Thanks for Listening*, an autobiographical observation on professional milestones and highlights. His life story, however, as learned from extensive interviews as well as published sources and the recollections of contemporaries, is that of an outgoing Depression-era youth whose teachers and other mentors encouraged his pursuit of ambitious goals. Throughout his career Brickhouse combined diligence and friendly confidence with a continual involvement in the rapid technological advancements that followed his early years in radio.

Sportswriters and speakers often use the word *legendary* in describing Brickhouse. Indeed his career has been marked by works of legend: more major-league baseball telecasts than any other announcer; interviews with six presidents and, among countless others, with John Barrymore, Babe Ruth, and Joe Louis—both before and after the Brown Bomber became the world heavyweight boxing champion. Brickhouse was the first announcer on WGN-TV and the first television broadcaster for the basketball Chicago Bulls.

After Brickhouse retired from the Chicago Cubs telecasts in 1981, his lengthy career was summarized by a close friend, WGN sports editor Jack Rosenberg: "When they write the final history of twentieth-century broadcasting, he will go down as one of the all-time greats because he has done it all. He's done sports, he's done barn dances, he's done political conventions, he's done after-dinner speaking."

More than a decade since Rosenberg's assessment Brickhouse continues an active public life—not particularly involving sports events but more in support of civic and charitable organizations—still manifesting the work ethic and innate optimism that characterized his broadcasting career.

For assistance in this biography I am grateful to Mr. Brickhouse for hours of interviews and for permitting access to his personal papers and WGN-TV office files. Others gave generously of their time as well; information from those sources is found throughout the narrative. For the research, especially regarding sports, I was helped by the staff at several organizations and institutions, including the Chicago and Peoria public libraries, Bradley University library, the Museum of Broadcast Communications, and the archives of both the National Baseball Hall of Fame and *The Sporting News*. The staff of the Rochester, Illinois, public library provided excellent service in filling interlibrary loan requests.

The assistance of my friend and mentor Ellen Whitney was invaluable. She recommended improvements to the drafts and offered historical information. (In 1944 Ellen reported on the Illinois Republican Convention, as did Jack.) And my husband, John, merits special recognition for always being available as a computer tutor and in general giving advice and support.

Janice Petterchak

CHAPTER 1

Family

IN APRIL 1994 THREE LEGENDS OF THE CHICAGO CUBS returned to help celebrate the eightieth anniversary of Wrigley Field. Jack Brickhouse and his longtime colleagues Vince Lloyd and Lou Boudreau teamed with current Cubs broadcaster Harry Caray for an evening of baseball play-by-play and reminiscences. Observing the four men, Caray's partner Steve Stone remarked, "It's like watching Mount Rushmore."

Far longer than any other broadcaster, Jack Brickhouse was the radio and then the television voice of the Chicago Cubs. During his career he announced a variety of other events, but it is with the Cubs, the White Sox, and the Bears that sports fans most closely identify the Brickhouse name.

A self-described "product of Peoria's pool halls" during the Great Depression, John Beasley "Jack" Brickhouse could not have imagined the future beyond his adolescence in central Illinois. Seven generations earlier, in the mid-1600s, his German ancestor William Von Steinhousen, accompanied by his young British wife and three children, arrived in the United States and became a Virginia farmer. A great-great-grandson, Matthew Brickhouse, served in the War of 1812; one of his children, John Beasley Brickhouse, fought as an Alabama Confederate in the War Between the States.

John's fourteen-year-old son, John William "Will" Brickhouse, fascinated by the performance of a traveling vaudevillian hypnotist, ran away from his parents' Clarksville, Tennessee, home seeking work in the entertainment field. He made his way to Chicago, where he found jobs as a sideshow barker and a concessionaire at the White City amusement park. Then he began managing a chain of midwestern theater houses. His son would later relate, "My father owned shows, ran them, gave them away, won them in card games, lost them in card games." Will Brickhouse is credited with originating "split-week vaudeville," booking acts into small towns for two or three performances instead of the typical weeklong engagements. The change enabled entertainers to gain additional experience "in the sticks" that for many led to professional careers.

Eventually becoming a sales manager for the Pathe Film Exchange, Brickhouse traveled the Midwest selling and scheduling silent movies, the newest form of popular entertainment. His territory included Peoria, Illinois, where in 1915 he met and soon married Daisy James, the only child of Frank and Mae Webber James.

At the turn of the century the James family had emigrated from Cardiff, Wales, to Bureau County in north-central Illinois. Frank James worked at the St. Paul Mine in Cherry and in 1909 was one of the 259 men killed there in an explosion and fire—the worst mine disaster in the state's history.

Shortly after the tragedy the young widow Mae James moved with her daughter to Peoria, about fifty miles southwest of Cherry. Mae became a cook at Proctor Hospital, and fifteen-year-old Daisy, lying about her age, was hired as a cigar stand cashier at a downtown businessmen's hotel. There she met the "been everywhere, seen everything" film salesman from Chicago, Will Brickhouse. Within a month they were married. He was thirty-nine, she a "naive little unsophisticated immigrant" teenager.

On January 24, 1916, weeks before Daisy's sixteenth birthday, John Beasley "Jack" Brickhouse was born in Peoria's Methodist Hospital. The couple later separated, and in 1919 Will Brickhouse succumbed to pneumonia in Chicago. He was buried in his Tennessee hometown, near the grave of his father. "I really wish he had lived," Jack says, "because I think he and I would have had a lot in common."

In about 1920, Daisy Brickhouse wed Peorian Gilbert G. Schultze. The family lived with her mother at 515 Second Avenue and later at 311 Fisher Street, quiet residential areas near the thriving business district. Young Jack Brickhouse attended Lincoln Grammar School and after classes often walked to Proctor Hospital, where he helped carry food trays to the patients. "Being a typical kid, that was the way I got something extra to eat. I wasn't kidding anybody; they knew why I was helping out, but they didn't mind."

A better-than-average student academically, Jack's first love throughout grammar school was basketball. In the upper grades he played on the Lincoln school team.

They used to have a basketball court on the bricks outside school. For several years all I ever wanted for Christmas—the *only* gift I wanted—was a basketball, because if I owned the ball, the big kids would let me in the game. On those bricks the basketball would wear out every year; that's why I always wanted a new one. I actually got one for five or six straight years.

On the school team we had a big, tall black kid named Al Sperlock. Al and I became good buddies because he could get the ball and I could shoot. He'd feed it to me, I'd shoot, and in she'd go.

Brickhouse and his school friends "took to hanging around Woodruff Field," home of the Peoria Tractors, a minor-league baseball team in the Three-I (Illinois, Indiana, Iowa) League.

We always hoped a foul ball would come out of the ballpark so we could get it; then we'd run up to the gate and give it to the usher, and he'd let us in for free. Or, if we hung around until the seventh or eighth inning, he'd let us in anyway. Also, on open-ing day we could get out of school for the afternoon game, so naturally we'd go.

My heroes were guys nobody had heard of then and certainly will never hear of again: Babe Thomas, Big Bill Mazeur, Ollie Furman, Francis Duffy. They'd talk with me, sign autographs, give me a ball, pat me on the head.

Two players were prominent in Peoria. One was Ossie Bluege, who became a major-league player and manager for Washington. His little brother, Otto, also played pro ball, but the highest he went was the Peoria Tractors. I was there one opening day during grammar school when the game was held up for sev-eral minutes because Ollie Furman, the catcher, threw the ball so hard to little Otto Bluege at second base that he went up in the air and fell down—swallowing his chewing tobacco. The game was delayed while Otto recovered from swallowing that plug of tobacco. Funny the things you remember.

In 1927 the Peoria newspaper owners recruited "every kid they could find," including Jack, "to sell papers when Charles Lindbergh flew the Atlantic. The 'extra' edition was a big feature then—they sold like hotcakes." Jack stayed on as a newsboy, delivering papers in his neighborhood for just a week before deciding to move downtown.

I figured the more people, the more sales. In those days you sold both the *Journal* and the *Star*; you paid two cents for each paper, sold it for three cents, and kept the penny. With luck sometimes you'd get the whole nickel. I took a look at a couple of office buildings. One with a lot of traffic was the Jefferson Building. I thought, I'll just stand in the lobby, and when people come out from work, I'll sell them papers.

It was a good idea; it was so good that another guy had beat me to it. This big kid came over and said, "Hey, out of here, now! If you're back tomorrow, I'll kick your butt." Well, I brooded about it overnight and then figured, Hey, I've got as much right as that guy. I went back the next day, and sure enough, he kicked me. I ran one block to the police station and found a husky Irish cop, who probably had four or five kids of his own. I put on a good show, telling him in tears about being pushed around by this guy when all I was trying to do was earn money to help my mother.

The cop took me by the hand, and we went back to the building. He grabbed that kid by the scruff of his neck and said, "If you harm so much as a hair on this boy's head, before I throw you in jail, I'll beat the hell out of you." Well, my God, I owned that building.

Ever enterprising, Jack soon added a second clientele at the nearby Lehman Building. "Strangely, nobody else came in; I had a monopoly. And to peddle those papers, my mother made me wear a clean shirt and necktie."

During sixth grade he and his classmates sold pencils to buy a volleyball for the girls and a basketball for the boys.

One day after school I was heading up the street to pick up my newspapers. Along came a truck, so I raced to hop it. We kids did this and would ride for several blocks. That afternoon when I went after the truck, I lost my footing, fell, and broke my left wrist. Then I was walking around with my broken arm in a cast and a sling.

Well, I already was fairly well liked by the secretaries in the office buildings; when I appeared with my pencils in the sling, I couldn't get a big enough supply! I sold twice as many as the rest of the room combined. The pencils were a nickel; the customers were giving me dimes. I'd sell a pencil and a paper; they'd give me a quarter and tell me to keep the change. After the wrist was healed, they had a heck of a time getting the cast off my arm; I wanted to wear it for the rest of the year.

Admittedly, I was a schemer; apparently I had

inherited my father's sales ability. But I also learned from that experience—learned about being aggressive and taking advantage of opportunities. It really paid off. And that was the only time in all my school years that I was a teacher's pet—I couldn't do a thing wrong by Miss Ruth Tutt.

In 1929 Jack enrolled at Peoria Manual Training High School. He had given up selling newspapers to begin caddying with a friend at Mount Hawley Country Club (the beginning of a lifelong passion for golf). He was in the precollege curriculum and became a reporter for the school newspaper, *The Manual*. His favorite sport was still basketball. "I wound up being pretty good," at one time playing on five teams using three aliases to maintain his school eligibility. During his freshman year the Manual varsity team won the state basketball championship—a school achievement not repeated until 1994.

In his junior year Jack was named associate editor of *The Manual*. "The sports editor was a senior, Vernon Hammond. I wanted him to put in the word for me to succeed him when he graduated. I was playing politics with him and among other things took his sister—my first date—to the junior prom."

Active in dramatics throughout high school, Brickhouse "fell in love with broadcasting" during his junior year. He played the part of George Washington's half brother in a local radio program. "When I found out that by talking into a machine in Peoria, I could be heard all the way over the river in East Peoria, and even ten miles away in Pekin, I thought, This is a miracle—I want to be part of it!"

The gregarious Brickhouse was elected senior-class vice

president and won the assignment as sports editor of *The Manual*. He also captained the swimming team, represented the school in the National Forensic League state championship at Northwestern University, qualified for the National Honor Society, and garnered the lead role in the senior class play.

Near the time of his high school graduation, Daisy and Gilbert Schultze separated. A year later they were divorced. The marriage had been strained for some time, particularly over Schultze's relationship with his stepson. Jack remembers, "He didn't know the difference between love and mother love. He bounced me around a lot, but I was smart enough to know that if I complained I might threaten our security. I took it until I was seventeen, and one day when he whacked me, I whacked back. Daisy found out about it, and she knew she had to make a choice, the son or the husband. So once again it was Jack and Daisy and Mae—my little cockney grandmother."

In that summer of 1933 Jack and a friend, Kenneth Grieves, combined their savings of about $80 and hitchhiked around the Midwest. They traveled first to Chicago, attracted by advertisements for the Century of Progress world's fair. After viewing the various burlesque shows and carnival acts, the boys "had about eighty cents" for the rest of the trip. Hitchhiking again and sometimes hopping freight trains, they picked up caddying jobs along the way for spending money. Once they spent the night in a Kentucky jail after a policeman took them in for vagrancy.

Returning from the summer trip, Jack completed his plans for college, hoping to become a lawyer. During his senior year at Manual he had been one of several students recruited by Bradley Polytechnic Institute in Peoria.

I wanted to go to college very badly. We didn't have much money, so I obviously would need a job. I asked for and got a meeting with Dr. Frederic Hamilton, president of Bradley. I said: "Dr. Hamilton, I would love to attend Bradley. Can you get me some kind of employment that will enable me to pay my tuition?"

Dr. Hamilton assured me that I would have a job, so I went to the business office and signed up with the registrar. The tuition was $100 a semester. I did not have the money, but my mother co-signed for the tuition. Then she went to a loan company and borrowed another $25 so I could buy books. At that time there was a wonderful businessman in Peoria named Milo Reeve. He loved kids and helped as many as he could. I asked him to help me.

Reeve responded that he had already given out his funds for the year, but he offered to co-sign the college loan. Jack gratefully accepted. He began classes in the fall of 1933 and played forward on the Westminster Church YMCA and Bradley freshman basketball teams. An experienced swimmer, he and friend Rudolph Huber enrolled in an elementary swimming class for their physical education requirement. After the first session, thinking they were alone, the two freshmen swimmers raced the length of the pool, only to be confronted by their instructor, John "Dutch" Meinen—a former Bradley football star and later its athletic director. " 'I had no idea my teaching was so good,' Meinen remarked. Then he had Rudy and me teach that class the rest of the semester."

In addition to attending college, practicing basketball, and studying, Jack worked part-time as a dishwasher at the

Pere Marquette Hotel—and "lost twenty pounds on an already skinny frame." One Saturday, scheduled to work at the hotel until noon and then to compete in a Bradley swimming meet, Jack was told by his boss to remain and help prepare for an evening function. Jack tried to explain his school commitment but, when given an ultimatum to stay, he lost his temper, hit the man, and lost the job.

Then, as the weeks passed, he kept asking Bradley staff about the promise of campus work. President Hamilton did not meet with Jack or return his telephone calls. In the meantime, Jacob Lentz in the business office was pressing Jack for tuition payments. "I couldn't give money I didn't have, and finally at the end of the semester I had to drop out of college. I made a resolution to Mr. Lentz: 'The day will come when I'll have enough pocket money to pay this tuition; but I will not pay a penny as long as Dr. Frederic Hamilton is associated with the school.' I found out that the statute of limitations on debt collection was seven years, so I was determined to stall for at least that long."

In 1945, after Hamilton retired, Lentz would send Jack a letter informing him that Milo Reeve intended to pay the tuition "because he didn't want to go to his grave with this one black mark. Every other kid he helped had repaid." Jack immediately responded: "Now the bill will be paid. You will get a cashier's check from Daisy Brickhouse for the whole amount, including interest. My name will not be on the record, because while I was at Bradley Dr. Hamilton made no effort to square the situation with me."

Leaving college in late 1933, Jack took a job at the new Hiram Walker distillery, on the shore of the Illinois River. "My job was to fill bottles with gin and put them on an endless chain. The girl next to me capped the bottles, then other people down the line sealed, labeled, and packed them. Once in a while you had to suck on the siphon, and when you did, you got a mouthful of warm gin—which, of course, you were supposed to spit out. One day I decided to swallow a couple of swigs; before long, they had to call an ambulance. Naturally, I was fired, again."

Out of work and "hanging around" Peoria, Jack and his friend Kenneth Grieves decided to join the Civilian Conservation Corps, one of the Depression-era federal employment programs.

> As I recall, you were paid $30 a month—$25 you would have sent home, and $5 you could keep. You would be sent to Wyoming or South Dakota or someplace to break down trees in forests, or make roads, or whatever.
>
> We got on the train, and as it was pulling out of the Peoria station, heading for Jefferson Barracks, Missouri, I suddenly changed my mind and said, "Kenny, this is not for me." I jumped off the train; he stayed on. About three weeks later I was in the broadcasting business in Peoria.

CHAPTER 2

Young Man in Peoria

I N THE 1930S GREATER PEORIA—WHICH ENCOMPASSES East Peoria and Pekin across the Illinois River—was nearly as populous as Rockford, the state's second-largest city. Distillers, brewers, and farm implement manufacturers helped carry Peoria through the Depression, providing employment to residents throughout west-central Illinois. "Don't say we were a hick town, because we weren't," cautions Kenneth Jones, longtime sports editor of the *Peoria Journal*. In fact a few years later the *Saturday Evening Post* described Peoria as "the whiskey and earth-moving capital of the universe."

Jack was still in town in 1934 and still without a job or college funds. His friends, familiar with his gift of gab, urged him to enter an announcing contest at the local radio station, WMBD. The first prize was a $50 wristwatch. "I thought, Well, I'd been heavy on speech and dramatics in high school and in what little college I had. If I could win that watch, maybe I could cash it in and head for the West Coast, where there was a railroad strike. Times were tough; I decided I wanted to work even if the strikers didn't."

He won a preliminary round but finished fifth in the finals. "I think I beat the fifty-five-year-old man. And I knew why I didn't win. I fell on my face when asked to talk for two minutes about some tool I couldn't even identify. I found out quickly the importance of being able to ad-lib as a broadcaster."

Even though Jack took only fifth place, a WMBD staff member detected some talent in the teenage contestant's delivery. The station owner, Edgar Bill, gave Jack a tryout, and after two weeks of unpaid work he was invited to stay for another week. "I told him, 'Look, I've got a chance to get my job back at the hotel that fired me, and I need the money. My mother is supporting me, and she's making only about $15 a week.'"

So at the age of eighteen Brickhouse was offered his first job in radio—at a salary based on the National Recovery Act scale. He remembers Bill's plan: " 'We'll make you a half-time switchboard operator and a half-time announcer. You'll get $7 and $10; $17 for the week.' That was the most money I'd seen in my life. I was tickled pink, grabbed it—and in 1934 what was to become my lifetime career was born."

Jack joined several other announcers at the WMBD studio, on the second and third floors of the downtown Orpheum Theater. "The timing was very lucky for me. I needed help, and I got it. In those days in radio everybody had to do everything, and that included selling ads and sweeping the studio. For at least that first year I was a much better switchboard operator than I was a broadcaster."

WMBD had been established in 1927 and become affiliated with the Columbia Broadcasting System in 1931. Peoria already was recognized for such radio talent as Marian and

Jim Jordan—"Fibber McGee and Molly"—who began their careers there, as did Charles Correll, later to become Andy of "Amos 'n' Andy," once described as the "most listened-to individuals in the history of radio."

When Edgar Bill took over WMBD in 1931, he encouraged his staff to create and develop new programs.

> Bill knew that programming and product were the lifeblood of the business. And that was one of the great steps in early broadcasting, because, rather than go to the pool hall—and there was a pool hall, by the way, just around the corner—rather than spend time there between shows, we would stay and try to be creative.
>
> We had the chance not only to write but also to produce, perform, sell—all of it. Now, maybe ninety-nine of those ideas were worthless, but number one hundred would pay off. It was one of the most productive single periods in the lives of the people who worked there.
>
> In those days we did a tremendous amount of live programming, one show after another, a lot of local news, and since we were a CBS station, a lot of network wire service news. We all made plenty of mistakes, but we were able to learn from them, to help each other.

To Jack, Edgar Bill was a giant in the history of broadcasting, "an innovator, a visionary." As managing director of WLS radio in Chicago, one of his program creations had been a Saturday night "old fiddlers' contest," which devel-

oped into the famous "WLS Barn Dance"—with such per-
formers as Gene Autry, Pat Buttram, the Sons of the Pioneers,
and "Little Georgie" Gobel. When Bill moved to Peoria, he
produced a local version of the program and made Jack the
announcer. "The joke was I emceed so many barn dances I
wound up with a delivery that sounded like the g-string
twang on a guitar. But I loved them"—hosting both the
local show and the WLS troupe when it visited Peoria.

In April 1935, WMBD began an eighteen-hour schedule of
live broadcasts. Among the added programs were morning
reports from the Peoria weather bureau, described in the
Journal as "the only government weather bureau in the
United States equipped with a radio microphone." A federal
meteorologist, M. L. Fuller, gave his broadcasts from the
bureau office, several blocks from the station.

> Fuller was a real character, and he had no concept of
> time. The weather report was scheduled from 9:00
> to 9:05, when another show was to begin. The next
> thing you knew, it would be eight minutes after, and
> he would still be talking about some cumulus masses
> in Medicine Hat, Wyoming. Or Mrs. Fuller, an ardent
> gardener, would walk in, and you would hear her in
> the background: "Have you seen my garden shears?"
> "Now, hold it, Marian. Can't you see I'm on the
> air?" "Oh, beg your pardon."
>   Well, it was finally decided that M. L. Fuller was
> not modern enough, couldn't keep up with the times
> by observing schedules. They pulled him off and had
> a studio announcer give the weather report. I have
> seen complaint mail in my time, but none like that

which came when they took M. L. Fuller off the air. The whole of central Illinois got burned up. WMBD learned a lesson: that man was part of our family. They had to bring him back.

Many years after Jack's tenure at WMBD, he learned that his mother may have saved his job there:

She privately sought out Edgar Bill and told him that, like a lot of eighteen- and nineteen-year-olds, I had a trigger temper. (Actually, I had already gotten into a couple of fights, with a drunk pushing me around during a dance band broadcast and with another guy trying to grab the microphone for smart-aleck remarks.) Daisy said to Mr. Bill, "He probably comes by it honestly. His father had a temper, and I guess I have one, too. But I want to tell you that I have never seen this boy as happy as he is now. If he does get in a little trouble here and there, I think he'll grow out of it."

She said Bill told her, "Mrs. Brickhouse, it's been my experience that if a man has too much fighting spirit, it can be toned down a little. But if he doesn't have enough, you cannot give it to him. Don't worry about Jack; he'll be fine."

Bill's assistant manager and programming director, Gomer Bath, was to Jack "a brilliant man." In 1933 Bath originated and hosted a WMBD program called "Man on the Street," giving "every resident of central Illinois" the opportunity to express opinions on the radio. Bath eventually assigned the series to Jack, who went on to host "Man on the Street" six afternoons a week for more than five years.

> There was no taping, no seven-second delay. What you said went on the air, so you had to be a little careful about the people you talked to; we were embarrassed once in a while.
>
> Our sponsor was Loewenstein's Furniture Store on South Adams—a bit off the downtown path. In January and February, three people would come by in that fifteen minutes we were on the sidewalk with the subject of the day. And those three people didn't want to stop and talk to some young idiot out in the cold. I was constantly hauling Loewenstein's salesmen out on the street, giving them phony names and phony jobs and talking to them until somebody legitimate came by. The studio joke was that Jack Loewenstein would hire only salesmen who could do at least three dialects.

Later another WMBD announcer, Howard Dorsey, teamed with Jack for the daily sidewalk interviews. "We faked it like nobody in the world faked it. We did voices, characters, every nationality, every religion, every language, every job, all the trick voices we could invent until someone came along willing to be interviewed. In decent weather sometimes we had mobs. And that was the kind of training you wouldn't trade for anything."

Only three weeks after joining the WMBD staff, Jack covered his first sporting event. He had learned that a milkman, the friend of a station employee, was being paid by WMBD to broadcast area high school football games. Jack asked for the assignment as part of his duties.

> So they sent me out to Woodruff Field. My first game was between Manual and Hillsboro High. It was raining cats and dogs, and the field was muddy. I was standing behind the goalposts with all that heavy equipment on my back. Three minutes after the game began, the numbers on the uniforms were unreadable. I couldn't see a thing and missed a touchdown. Then, when the team kicked the extra point, I called it a field goal. I was so bad that one of the veteran announcers, Harry Luedeke, got on the streetcar, came out, and finished the game for me.
>
> I felt bad about it, but Edgar Bill called me in and gave me a great pep talk.

With determination he improved and then was assigned to a major heavyweight exhibition fight at the Majestic Theater between Willie Davis of Chicago and Detroit's Brown Bomber, Joe Louis. As an amateur light heavyweight, Louis had compiled a 17–4 record and by that time, according to Jack, "was gaining a lot of stature. He was knocking out everybody." Near the end of the second round of the scheduled four-round bout, "Joe hit Davis with a series of lefts and then a right, and Davis went down to stay."

Interviewing Louis on the radio after the fight, Jack noticed the twenty-year-old's facial hair, "that particular growth that kids get before they start to shave. I made mention of it: 'You haven't shaved yet, have you?'" The question and Louis's response—"Nope, I ain't gonna shave until I win the title," which happened two years later—were carried on a national wire service and published in the entertainment magazine *Variety*.

Beginning in 1935, Jack hosted "The Town Crier" six days a week, "informal dialogue" on civic activities in the area. Sunday morning assignments ranged from covering local worship services to reading the newspaper comics. "Milton Budd, the emcee of a very popular WMBD children's theater, also had been doing the funnies. One day he got sick, and I was asked to fill in. I read those Sunday funnies for a year and a half."

One June evening that year, a spectacular fire broke out at the Hiram Walker distillery. Jack stranded his date, called for radio equipment, and reported the $2.5 million disaster on WMBD from 8:00 P.M. to 10:00 the next morning. Thousands of barrels of whiskey spilled into the Illinois River, where men in rowboats "filled coal buckets and everything else to get some of the booze."

An often-told tale that Jack enjoys concerns a WMBD interview with a legendary actor.

It was a momentous occasion in Peoria when the great John Barrymore arrived to appear in *My Dear Children*. I was extremely apprehensive about what was to be a live interview on WMBD. As a young product of Peoria's pool halls, I had never seen a professional stage play. So my first question to this world-famous—but totally inebriated—member of the First Family of the American Theater went like this: "Sir, before you got into the movies, what was your background as an actor? Were you on the stage or anything?"

Barrymore almost sobered up. He paralyzed me with a baneful stare, then said in measured, icy tones, "Young man, ask me that question again, and my answer will probably cause your station to lose its license!"

Other WMBD assignments included the basketball games of Manual, Central, Spalding, and Woodruff high schools in Peoria, as well as East Peoria, Pekin, and other area schools. In 1936 the Manual team advanced to the state championship series in Champaign. At that time the exclusive tournament broadcast station was at the University of Illinois, with other stations permitted only to carry the public radio WILL feed. Jack again: "You couldn't do your own pickup, nor could you have commercials. Well, first, I wanted to broadcast those games. We'd been covering Manual all year; couldn't the team have the privilege of its own broadcasters? And second, I felt the rule was unjust. In the American way of life, what would be wrong with having the games sponsored?"

Jack discussed the situation with the man he calls "the father I never had," Kenneth Jones at the *Peoria Journal*. Jones agreed with Jack and suggested contacting H. V. Porter, an Illinois High School Association executive: "Why don't you ask Porter what happened to that $100,000 IHSA sinking fund?" Jack telephoned him at the association office in Chicago, requesting permission to broadcast the tournament. When Porter said no, Jack brought up Jones's question. "I didn't know what a sinking fund was—and I'm still not sure—but I was assertive anyway. 'There may be nothing wrong, but on the other hand, the implication is possible mismanagement. What happened to the $100,000 sinking fund? What if we asked that question on the air?' Porter paused, uttered an expletive, then gave us permission to broadcast the games."

Jack reports that the annual state championship series is now covered by twenty to thirty stations, "which is as it should be."

From time to time he broadcast baseball games of the Peoria Tractors in the Three-I League, teams he had followed since grammar school days. One of the stars in 1934 was a seventeen-year-old infielder, Phil Cavarretta, who debuted while still a senior at Chicago's Lane Technical High School. The day after pitching a no-hit, no-run game in the American Legion state championship, Cavarretta signed with the Cubs, who assigned him to the Peoria farm club. Jack was the broadcaster for Cavarretta's first game: "Phil hit for the cycle: single, double, triple, homer. We knew we weren't going to keep *this* guy very long. Sure enough, a short time later he was moved up to Reading in the Pennsylvania league, then finished the season in Chicago and never did go back to the minors.

"A sidelight: While Cavarretta was in Peoria, he fell in love with a beautiful little dancer named Lorraine. We were all in love with Lorraine, but Phil won her. Theirs is one of the great marriages of all time."

When not working at the station, Jack enjoyed listening to broadcasts of the Cubs and White Sox on WGN from Chicago, with Bob Elson the broadcaster for both teams. "He was the scout on the frontier drive, a pioneer . . . the most imitated, creative baseball broadcaster who ever lived," Jack told author Curt Smith in *Voices of the Game*, a chronicle of major-league broadcasters. Unlike the hapless Cubs of recent years, the team in the 1930s consistently finished at or near the top of the National League. "Every kid on the block knew the Cubs had to win the pennant every three years—

like clockwork. They won in 1929, in '32, in '35, in '38. To us in Peoria it was almost providential." Through promotional visits to Peoria, Elson became acquainted with the local sports announcer. A few years later, Elson and Brickhouse would become partners in Chicago.

Continuing the popular "Man on the Street" interviews with Howard Dorsey, Jack also hosted other variety and dramatic series, including "Moskin's Radio Theater of the Air" and dance band programs from local nightclubs. As broadcaster for "The Last Minute Sports Review," he was complimented by the *Journal* for "vivid, fast-moving descriptions of sports events. . . . His interviews with notables of football, basketball, baseball, wrestling, boxing, and other sports are also familiar to fans in this vicinity."

Moving from the Orpheum Theater to larger quarters in the Alliance Building, WMBD in the spring of 1936 constructed and dedicated a 254-foot transmitter between Peoria and Pekin, on the banks of the Illinois River. And Jack—by then director of sports and special features—decided to climb the transmitting tower for a live radio description of the river valley landscape.

His daring adventure was covered as a front-page story in the *Journal*: several hundred motorists "gathered on the premises to watch the ascent, which was climaxed by a 15-minute broadcast by Brickhouse at the top of the tower." An accompanying photograph showed Jack halfway up the tower, without a safety net, carrying "25 or 35 pounds of equipment strapped to his back." Jack recalls that because of the traffic jam around the site "Governor Henry Horner's arrival for the dedication was delayed for nearly forty-five minutes."

In the 1936–37 basketball season the freshman team at Bradley Polytechnic Institute had, according to Jack,

"mopped up the varsity in practice." Confident of his players' potential, coach Alfred J. "Robbie" Robertson arranged
the 1937–38 schedule against several big-name schools,
including Yale, Oregon, and Southern Methodist University.
Their coaches "thought they could use Bradley as a door-
mat." The schedule also included Illinois Wesleyan University in Bloomington, Millikin University in Decatur, and
Knox College in Galesburg, all strong teams in the Little
Nineteen Conference. And Jack wanted to broadcast Bradley's games on WMBD:

> However, as a CBS station WMBD was committed to
> carrying the network shows of Bing Crosby, Kate
> Smith, Paul Whiteman, Eddie Cantor, and others. We
> couldn't knock them off the air for Bradley basket-
> ball, so the program director and I proposed to
> record the games and broadcast them after the ten
> o'clock news. The sales manager and one or two
> others at our program meeting said, "Do you think
> people will actually listen to the broadcast of a game
> when they know how it ended? It won't work." I sug-
> gested that we conduct a poll—ask the people how
> they felt about it. The bosses made one mistake; they
> let me conduct the poll.
>
> I stood on the corner of Main and Jefferson in
> Peoria, and all of the first ten people I talked to said
> no, they didn't think they'd be interested. I threw
> those in a sewer and went to my favorite pool hall,
> the Saratoga, and filled out a hundred ballots. Sixty-
> three of those people said yes, they'd be interested;
> about twenty-two said no; and the rest were unde-
> cided. On the strength of that poll we got a trial

broadcast. We got to do the Bradley-Louisville game
at the Peoria Armory.

Our little station didn't own any recording equipment, so we borrowed some thirty-three-inch recording disks from a hobbyist, Norris Bouchelle. They
must have weighed two hundred pounds; you could
see the table sag at courtside. We recorded the game,
and it turned out to be a Bradley blowout, something
like 71–26. Two or three times during the broadcast
I said, "Now, you listeners probably know the final
score, but because of network commitments, this is
the only way we can bring you the Bradley games. If
you want us to continue, will you please let us
know?"

We broke the station's record for mail response:
within the next forty-eight hours we had letters, post-
cards, telegrams delivered by hand, petitions from
Legion posts, the VFW, churches, labor organizations,
school kids—everybody saying, "Boy, that was great!
We want the games, all of them!"

Thus, by autumn of 1937—three years after he began
working as a half-time announcer—Jack's primary broadcast
association was with sports. As he says, "On the strength of
a phony poll a lucky career was born."

He broadcast all of the Bradley games, barnstorming
with the Braves from the West Coast to Washington, D.C.,
and in nearby towns and Chicago. Known as the Famous
Five, the talented team compiled a 52–9 record from 1936
through 1939 and went undefeated in conference competition.
Most of the home games were sellouts, and tickets often went
at premium prices. According to Bradley graduate Bob Leu,

one theater owner "noted the excitement over the Brick-house broadcasts of these recent conquests, knocked off the late feature movie at the downtown Palace, and before a blank screen piped in the play-by-play to the delight of its patrons."

Years later *Peoria Journal Star* sports editor Paul King recalled how he and his dad had listened to Jack's "voice coming out of our big old radio. The station used to warn people just before it gave the final score to precede the broad-cast, and if you wanted you could turn down the sound and thus not know who had won until the end of the game." Another Peorian remembered: "The Bradley rebroadcast would be heard on practically every street in the city. And this is no exaggeration, hard to believe though it is today."

Closing the 1937–38 season with a 19–1 record and ranked thirteenth of 550 college and university teams, the Bradley Braves were selected to play in the first National Invi-tational Tournament, sponsored by the Metropolitan New York Basketball Writers Association. The popular Braves broadcaster accompanied his jubilant team to New York City. "You think that wasn't something, when a little bitty school from a little bitty town with a little bitty station did a broadcast from Madison Square Garden?" The radio cov-erage was sponsored by Caterpillar Tractor, Keystone Steel & Wire, People's Federal Savings and Loan, and the Peoria Water Works Company. "Our gag was that Peoria was the one town where the water works needed advertising, because of the competition from Hiram Walker's Distillery and Pabst Brewery.

"The tournament was a big thing in Peoria. The team made the newspaper society page, and fans organized radio listening parties. At the Palace Theater, the movie was inter-rupted for the game broadcast. It was a fantastic period."

Though losing to Temple University in the first round of the finals, Bradley came home with the third-place trophy. One Braves fan, Rose M. Wood of nearby Elmwood, wrote to WMBD after the tournament, "I heard Jack the evening he was in the contest for announcers. He was good then and is surely going places with the sports events. I thought the broadcast of the Bradley-Temple game grand. I really almost sat on the edge of the chair hoping that Bradley would find that basket, and they did, but not enough. . . . Thanking you so much for all the good programs, and trusting . . . that Jack does not take life too seriously."

In 1939 the Bradley Braves compiled another winning record. Ranked seventeenth nationally, the team again was selected for the NIT. A special train carried fans from Peoria to New York, where the Braves repeated their third-place finish. Jack reflected years later that of the many basketball teams he covered in his career "few had the talent of those Bradley Braves."

Jack was also assigned to broadcast the football games of the University of Illinois and other Big Ten teams. In 1939 the Fighting Illini, 3–4–1 under veteran coach Robert C. Zuppke, defeated the conference champion Michigan. Says Jack: "Zuppke had one great talent; he was the best pointer in the world. What I mean is, he would assess his ball club before the season, then point at one game on the schedule. 'Whatever happens in the season, we're going to win that game. This year I'm pointing at Michigan, because they're the defending champions. Besides, beating Michigan is fun. We'll prepare for all the other games as well, but Michigan is the one I want.' The Illinois 16–7 win over Tom Harmon, Forest Evashevski, and company was one of the great upsets in Big Ten history."

An incident late in the year in Bloomington, some forty

miles from Peoria, showed Jack's own increasing popularity
and his influence on central Illinois sports. When Illinois
Wesleyan University fired its football coach and athletic director, Harry Bell, the announcement was made by the *Bloomington Pantagraph* sports editor, Fred "Brick" Young. Jack
was convinced that Young, "one of the most powerful and
influential of the downstate sports editors," was responsible
for Bell's dismissal. "I resented the fact that Wesleyan would
permit the local sports editor to do the firing, and I went on
the air with the story."

The controversy spread throughout central Illinois, on
radio and in area newspapers. When Jack continued discussing the incident on WMBD, Wesleyan officials announced
that they would not permit the broadcast of an upcoming
Bradley-Wesleyan basketball game if he was assigned as the
announcer. "They claimed that I had done a biased broadcast of the Bradley-Wesleyan football game the previous fall,
which Wesleyan won. In those days there was no tape, not
even a wire recording. All we had were those great big disks,
which we didn't use very often, so there was no record of
what I had said."

WMBD attorney O. P. Westervelt responded in a lengthy
letter to Wesleyan president W. E. Shaw. After detailing some
of the issues, including the university's criticism of Brickhouse, Westervelt asked for a meeting to resolve "this unfortunate controversy":

> I knew Jack when he was a harum scarum young
> boy who used to spend most of his time at the
> YMCA when he was not in school. He is a self made
> young fellow and the radio listeners in Peoria sim-
> ply swear by Jack Brickhouse. I have listened to
> his broadcast of the sports events hundreds of

times and I have never heard anything that
smacked of partisanship or unfairness to either
side of the contest that he was broadcasting—in
fact, his enthusiasm and fairness are his two pre-
dominant qualities.

He is also rather expert in his ability to por-
tray an athletic contest so that the listener feels
that he is actually witnessing the contest itself. A
year ago there was rumor that a large Chicago
station had contracted with him to come to
Chicago as an announcer and I well recall how
excited the Peoria public became over this news,
and how relieved they were when they learned that
Jack was not going to leave Peoria.

Westervelt also responded to a second Wesleyan condition, that WMBD pay $100 to broadcast the game: "I know
that this local station, with Mr. Brickhouse announcing, has
announced dozens of basketball games the past two winters
from cities all over the country and they never have been
asked to pay any such charge."

Edgar Bill and Jack attended a meeting on the issue at
Wesleyan. WMBD had loyal support from Bradley, whose
athletic director, A. J. Robertson, discussed canceling the
game. Eventually President Shaw mediated a compromise:
Jack would be allowed to broadcast the game for a $25
WMBD contribution to the university's athletic fund. Accord-
ing to him, "That may have been the first time in the United
States that a station paid to broadcast an athletic event.
Compare that to the millions paid today."

By then Jack was a popular guest speaker on the prep-
sports banquet circuit. In the spring of 1938 he was featured
at the nearby Fairview High School basketball awards program. The local newspaper reported that during Jack's speech

the male parents and friends among the two hundred in attendance suddenly rose "as one individual and dashed for the exits, leaving Jack standing, an amazed look on his face." He thought he was the victim of a prank until the master of ceremonies announced, "It's a fire alarm."

According to the newspaper, "The blaze in a nearby garage was quickly extinguished and the volunteer firemen returned to listen as Jack finished his speech." He added, "I appreciate that you trusted me enough to leave me alone with your women." Afterward he told the reporter, "I've had 'em walk out on me one or two at a time, but this is the first time an audience left en masse."

Daisy and Jack were saddened in 1938 by the death of Daisy's seventy-two-year-old mother, Mae Webber James. Jack remembers Mae as "quite a lovely lady. She had diabetes, but she died after breaking her hip and contracting pneumonia. To the last day she never lost her cockney accent."

In 1939 Jack initiated a weekly program on WMBD, "Here's How They Did It," fifteen-minute interviews with prominent area businessmen. In a deep baritone the twenty-three-year-old introduced each of the segments as "life stories of men who made their place in the world through fortitude, patience, and the ability to capitalize on breaks." He dedicated his series "to the inspiration and encouragement of the younger people in our listening audience."

Jack credits Edgar Bill with advice that became the foundation of his own career. Noticing that Jack sometimes changed his delivery style in imitation of other broadcasters, Bill advised, "The public can tell sincerity. Instead of copying others, be the best Jack Brickhouse." Jack adds, "I think I have passed on that advice to a thousand kids."

As the broadcaster for Bradley and Big Ten sports, Three-I baseball, "several hundred, maybe a thousand" Golden Gloves and other boxing contests, high school sports events, and a schedule of daily programs, Brickhouse enjoyed his celebrity status and was the subject of frequent press stories. In the summer of 1939 he and his girlfriend Nelda Teach vacationed in Wisconsin with two other couples. A native of nearby Avon, Illinois, Nelda had attended the University of Illinois and the Gem City Business College in Quincy. She met Jack at the Lincoln Loan Company in Peoria, when he financed his first automobile, a used Willys sedan. Nelda was the firm's secretary and notary public.

> During the vacation we decided to get married. Michigan had a state law authorizing a waiver on the usual three-day waiting period. I think the provision was designed for expectant parents, because the couple could put any date on the marriage license. We got a probate judge out of bed in Bessemer, Michigan, and his ten-year-old son was our witness. The judge was a little surprised when he asked the date we wanted on the license and I asked, "What day is it?" He raised his eyebrow and said, "Well, it's August 7."

Back in Peoria the *Journal-Transcript* reported on the marriage as "the most exciting news of the week." Later in the year Jack again broadcast the Bradley basketball games. The local newspapers also reported that he was interviewing for positions and assignments in Chicago but concluded that he would remain at WMBD. The situation changed several months later, at the end of the basketball season.

CHAPTER 3

On to Chicago

FROM FREQUENT PROMOTIONAL VISITS TO PEORIA, BOB Elson, WGN's popular Chicago White Sox and Cubs broadcaster, was well acquainted with Brickhouse and aware that he wanted to advance his career in a larger radio market. On March 14, 1940, during White Sox spring training on the West Coast, Elson sent Jack the following telegram:

> Have recommended you for our announcers staff and sports assistant   Expect a call   Wire me developments   Town House   Los Angeles Remember if asked you have a thorough knowledge of baseball   Regards   Bob Elson.

On the strength of Elson's recommendation, Jack was invited to Chicago for a WGN audition. Station manager Quin Ryan interviewed him for a position of staff announcer and assistant to Elson. On March 28, Ryan's assistant, Myrtle Stahl, sent Jack an offer "to have you join us on a leave-of-absence basis from your present position. . . . come in on Sunday, April 14th to learn our routine and go on schedule, Monday—April 15th. We plan to pay you $55.00 per week which figures $460.00 more per year than you are receiving at present."

Jack responded immediately, "I shall be there Sunday, April 14th to learn the routine, and be prepared to go to work Monday the 15th. The salary is very satisfactory, and I am looking forward to a mighty enjoyable change." Thus, after six years and some twenty thousand WMBD broadcasts, Jack Brickhouse and his wife, Nelda, moved from Peoria to Chicago for a staff announcing job with what he considered "one of the best stations in the country."

WGN had begun transmission in 1922 as WDAP. In 1924 the *Chicago Tribune* purchased the station and changed the call letters to WGN for the familiar *Tribune* slogan, "World's Greatest Newspaper." Almost immediately WGN began broadcasting sports events, including play-by-play of the Chicago Cubs, the only major-league team that permitted radio coverage of all of its games. The earliest broadcasters included both Elson and Ryan. In 1934 WGN joined with three other stations to form a cooperative network, the Mutual Broadcasting System. In 1940, the year Brickhouse was hired, WGN began a twenty-four-hour programming schedule. He recalls:

> Quin Ryan, the WGN manager, was one of the great radio pioneers. He had broadcast a World Series and was the exclusive announcer at the 1925 Scopes trial. The first year I was in Chicago, at six bucks a pop for a fifteen-minute show, I filled in for Quin on his news broadcasts.
>
> This was when the American Federation of Radio Artists was just beginning, and I wasn't yet a mem-

ber. Some broadcasters on our staff, like Spencer Allen and Guy Savage, helped organize AFRA. Quin could no longer assign his shows to other broadcasters as part of their shifts; he had to pay $6 each time from his own money. He was so angry with them that he said, "Have Brickhouse do my shows," which included Christmas, New Year's, his birthday, his wife's birthday, and so on. I made an extra $450 that first year, which was a good chunk of change in those days.

There were fifteen announcers at WGN, because there was a lot of live local programming. Being low man on that totem pole, I had the bad shift, which meant I signed off the place. I'd work until 1:30 in the morning, which was all right with me; I did not—still don't—like to get up early.

In the late 1930s and the 1940s Chicago was a major city on the Big Band dance circuit. WGN and the Mutual network helped popularize the music, assigning three tuxedoed announcers nightly, Jack among them, to broadcast the bands playing in Chicago:

One of WGN's sponsors was Bond Clothes, so Quin Ryan arranged for us to buy our tuxedoes there, at $5 down and a couple of dollars a week.

On the dance band broadcasts I would do a half hour at, we'll say, the Aragon Ballroom with Dick Jurgens when Eddie Howard was his vocalist. The second announcer would be ready at Otto Roth's Blackhawk Restaurant, with Ted Weems when Perry

Como was his vocalist. The third announcer would be getting ready in the Empire Room at the Palmer House with Eddy Duchin. I would do my half hour, giving me a full hour to get to my next assignment, at the Trianon Ballroom, to set up with Lawrence Welk. We'd start at 8:00 or 9:00 at night or, at the latest, 10:00, to 1:30 in the morning.

And then, at what is now the Hilton Hotel—then the Stevens Hotel—was Chuck Foster or Del Courtney, and then back to the Palmer House, maybe with "Your host, the toast of the coast, Griff Williams"; up to the Edgewater Beach, with Jan Garber. Those were fun assignments; I really enjoyed them.

In 1940 *Downbeat* magazine listed nearly eight hundred dance bands playing either one-night markets or extended hotel and ballroom engagements. Chicago was identified as "the hottest spot in the nation for band-building via radio." There and throughout the country, couples hosted dances in their homes—with radio music from the leading dance bands.

With World War II the mood of the country changed, yet the big bands remained popular. New radio station regulations were designed to prevent the Axis enemies from hearing potentially useful information. For the dance broadcasts only designated announcers—but no song dedications or weather descriptions—were permitted.

One evening at the Palmer House the popular bandleader and pianist Eddy Duchin took the microphone and dedicated songs to some of his friends. After the broadcast Jack warned him about the wartime restrictions, but Duchin countered, "Your station needs me more than I need you."

WGN station manager Frank Schreiber was determined that if Duchin repeated his use of the microphone, "We'll pull him off the air and pick up the Weems band at the Blackhawk." The following evening when Duchin was again uncooperative, Jack and his engineer abruptly ended the Palmer House broadcast. "But the word was around about Duchin; one employee called him 'insufferable.' Later that night Weems recognized me at the Blackhawk and introduced me to the audience as 'the guy who pulled the plug on Duchin.'" Eventually Jack came to admire Duchin, who as a navy lieutenant "was a genuine war hero."

As assistant to Bob Elson, Jack also soon began broadcasting Chicago Cubs and Chicago White Sox games.

My knowledge of baseball at that time consisted of having worked Three-I League games in Peoria. But Elson and guys like Pat Flanagan and Hal Totten working for the other stations (in those days there were several stations broadcasting the games) helped a young guy like me get started. After the game we would sit around the press quarters or somewhere, and they would give me tips—even though we were competitors.

The newspaper men, on the other hand, were not all that friendly immediately, and not without some reason. In the early days of broadcasting the newspaper reporter, who was dedicated to doing a good job chronicling sports, got about $45 a week—some maybe up to $50. Along came this thing called radio, and a guy with a voice that appealed to the public— and in some cases couldn't spell *baseball*—was broadcasting it. He would take material from the newspaper and use it on the air. And these broadcasters made a lot more money.

I was determined when I came up to keep my mouth shut, listen to and learn from the newspaper guys, and try to prove that not all broadcasters are plagiarists. I did it for the whole first year and eventually was accepted.

To give you an idea of how the newspapers felt about radio, they originally refused to print the broadcasting schedules. They recognized radio as two things: (1) a threat and (2) something that wasn't much of a threat; maybe it would die out. Eventually they found out that the radio listings were among the most widely read entries in the paper, so they had to print them. Otherwise the competition would do it.

Already a recognized announcer from the Bradley basketball games, Jack gained increasing identification with sports broadcasting as a result of the baseball games. Then, in the fall of 1940, he was assigned to Notre Dame football. The first game was at Chicago's Soldier Field against College of the Pacific. Among the stadium fans that day was Hollywood actor Ronald Reagan, who, according to the *Tribune* had "had a go at pro football with the Chicago Bears, but wasn't heavy enough, then on station WHO in Des Moines, Iowa, had not only covered football, but announced Cubs and White Sox games from Western Union tapes." During the Notre Dame game Brickhouse invited Reagan to the booth to cobroadcast a quarter and promote his new movie, *Knute Rockne, All American*. President Reagan remembered the occasion, Jack says, during a 1981 White House interview.

At WGN, senior announcer Pierre Andre recommended young Jack and other junior broadcasters for commercial assignments, "which brought an extra $25." His first such opportunity—reminiscent of Peoria—was a big-city version of "Man on the Street," live interviews from the Chicago Theater on State Street:

> I was at WGN in Tribune Tower. Guy Savage, who did the show, couldn't make it one day, and on fast notice I was told to do it. I took a cab; the fare was thirty-five cents. I gave the driver fifty cents, and when I got back I turned in for that half a buck.
>
> Myrtle Stahl, who ran Quin Ryan's office and consequently on occasion ran the station, called me to her office: "What is this?" I said, "It was raining. I've got two suits; one is in the cleaner's; one I just took out of the cleaner's, and I'm wearing it. The cab ride cost me thirty-five cents, and I gave the man fifty cents." She said, "Mr. Brickhouse, you could have gotten there by bus." I said, "Within a block, yes, if I wanted to walk the last block in the rain." She answered, "Mr. Brickhouse, the *Chicago Tribune* and WGN are not responsible for acts of God or nature. I will allow you bus fare, ten cents." That's the way things were in 1940 at WGN.
>
> But what an interesting cross section of people came along for "Man on the Street." That had to be the greatest education a young man could get. Remember, in those days there was no delay button in case someone used profanity or said something really improper. Yet I cannot remember one serious incident in all those shows.

WGN also had a lot of kids shows, soap operas, dramas. On one murder mystery program the lead character was a young radio actor named Mike Wallace, now with "60 Minutes" in New York. I was the commercial announcer.

During World War II programs relating to the war effort often were integrated into the WGN schedule. One of Jack's assignments was broadcasting from Fort Sheridan, where he "pitched the questions fielded by soldiers and sailors" in the sports quiz "Play Ask-It Ball," created by WGN program producer Paul Fogarty. With a new mobile-unit automobile, Jack also broadcast from a submarine plant at Manitowoc, Wisconsin, and interviewed military personnel on a B-17 Flying Fortress.

In August 1942 he participated in a unique experiment, the first large-scale blackout of an American city. According to the *Tribune*, the objective of the war simulation was to determine whether the Chicago area, "industrially one of the most vital to the country," could "make itself invisible to Axis bombers." The test territory of twelve million in population included northern Illinois, southern Wisconsin, and portions of Michigan. Streets, homes, offices, industrial buildings, and hotels were "thrown into full darkness"—even the downtown Holy Family Church, where the lights had burned continuously since the structure survived the 1871 Chicago fire.

WGN described the half-hour blackout from both an American Airlines passenger plane and the roof of the Chicago Board of Trade. Jack was aboard the DC-3 with naval officers and civil defense workers, broadcasting their observations of the experiment. "The point of the blackout," he said, "was to learn whether the enemy would be able to see the shore versus the land versus the water. If so, how should Chicago and the U.S. prepare?"

The *Tribune* reported that Chicago mayor Edward J. Kelly "watched the city disappear" from atop the Board of Trade. With him were the police commissioner, military and civil defense personnel, and newspaper and radio reporters, all wearing, according to the newspaper, "phosphorescent patches on their foreheads to prevent collisions in the dark." To Jack,

> It turned out to be an unusual broadcast; it was fascinating to see the city of Chicago totally blacked out. There was an occasional little flicker, but for the most part everybody—millions of people—cooperated. From the airplane I flipped the broadcast to the Board of Trade. The announcer asked the obvious question: "What is your impression, Mayor Kelly?" "What do you think is my impression? It's dark as hell up here." It's all he could think to say.
>
> NBC also described the blackout, with, I think, Dave Garroway in their plane. We found out later that there was a little mix-up in the instructions and in that darkness the two planes came within a couple hundred feet of each other.

Although baseball players faced the same military obligations as other American men, President Franklin D. Roosevelt decided that the sport was important to national morale. Writing to baseball commissioner Judge Kenesaw Mountain Landis in January 1942, Roosevelt stated that he did not want the schedules canceled as they had been during World War I: "I honestly feel that it would be best for the country to keep baseball going. There will be fewer people unemployed, and everybody will work longer hours and harder than ever before, and that means they ought to have a chance for recreation and for taking their minds off their work even more than before."

In the summer of 1942 Bob Elson took leave from WGN to join the navy. Brickhouse, already a familiar voice as Elson's assistant on both Cubs and Sox games, was assigned full-time to finish the 1942 season—"a dream come true," he said at the time. He also did news broadcasts and the autumn season of Big Ten football.

Among his basketball assignments, Jack recalls a 1942 public address role at a DePaul game that featured the debut of a "big, gangly center named George Mikan." When Jack introduced the 6'10" sophomore at Chicago Stadium, Mikan "actually tripped over his own feet, stumbled, and lost his balance—and the legend was born." Jack continued:

> The DePaul coach was Ray Meyer, who had been captain of the Notre Dame basketball team in both his junior and senior years. For a while after graduation he was an assistant to his coach, George Keogan. George Mikan from Joliet, Illinois, one of the first "physical giants" in sports, wanted to play basketball at Notre Dame. But Keogan misjudged the potential of this huge, clumsy, uncoordinated youngster and didn't accept him.
>
> Then Mikan enrolled at DePaul, and the job Meyer did in developing Mikan is legendary. For a long time Ray wouldn't let him shoot the ball, instead making him concentrate on learning to handle it. Ray

arranged private ballet lessons and ordered a face guard to protect Mikan's glasses because of his very poor eyesight.

Mikan was a tremendously willing student who believed in his coach and tried to do everything Ray told him. Mikan went on to a professional career and was voted the greatest basketball player of the first half of this century. And that is one of my favorite stories.

During the war Jack even became a cartoon character in the *Chicago Tribune*'s syndicated "Harold Teen" comic strip, depicted as radio announcer Jackson Brickhouse emceeing war-loan rallies. By 1943 Jack was already among the leading sports broadcasters in the nation, and Nelda helped answer the several hundred fan letters he received each week. Relieved of the Big Band duties, he was assigned to a full season of Cubs and White Sox home games, as well as daily news and sports shows, horse racing, and a weekly entertainment program.

On days when neither Chicago baseball team was at home, Jack broadcast the road games by Western Union ticker tape from the WGN studio.

The ticker days were fun, because we got to be a little creative. All we got on the tape would be, for instance, B1H, meaning ball one high; B2L, ball two low. We would look at the tape, which might read: "Jones singles to right; Smith singles to left." It gave us a chance sometimes to sound like geniuses. Knowing that Jones had singled to right, we could say, "You know, the last time Jones was up, that pitcher

got him out with a high inside curveball. But if he
curves him again, Jones may be ready for him this
time." Well, we already knew what happened. "Here
comes the pitch; whoa, there goes a base hit to right
field. High inside curve, and Jones hits it." Sometimes
we'd add to the broadcast with a sound effects record
that had crowd noise and a guy yelling "peanuts,
popcorn" and so forth.

Every once in a while we would warn our listeners: "If you're, say, at a bar next to a guy who offers,
'I'll bet you the next guy gets on base,' don't bet him.
He might know the Western Union code and be hearing it in the background." We would alert the audience to things like that.

As the 1943 baseball season ended, Jack and a Peoria
school friend, Maurice Fulton, decided to enlist in the Marine
Corps rather than wait for the expected draft notice. Jack
had been offered a navy rating and an army commission, but
both were in public relations and broadcasting. "I didn't
want to be in the announcing business for $25 a month or
$100 a month. I decided if I was taking time from a career,
I wanted to learn something—a foreign language or intelligence work, for example."

After the final Cubs game of 1943, Fulton and Brickhouse
left for service in the Marine Corps. "My highest rank as a
marine was when for three days I was an acting PFC. I was
in charge of the group in Chicago going to San Diego to boot
camp, because I was the oldest guy in the bunch. In order to
be in charge I had to rank them, so all the time we were on
that train I was an acting PFC."

Together in boot camp and joined by fellow recruit
William Veeck, Jr., of Chicago, the friends were separated

when medical tests revealed scar tissue on Jack's lungs from undiagnosed childhood tuberculosis. He was admitted to the navy hospital in San Diego, where the tuberculosis was initially diagnosed as moderately advanced and active but later was shown as "incipient, arrested." Even so, after two months he received his discharge. "At the time I swore if I ever got out of the service I'd never get up early again, and I've been about as good as my word ever since—not counting golf dates."

Awaiting the discharge, Jack was offered liberty to perform in the weekly Marine Corps "Halls of Montezuma" program on national radio. He played the commanding officer of Hollywood actor Pat O'Brien, "doing a guest appearance. We developed a friendship that lasted many years."

By act of Congress, discharged servicemen were allowed forty days to return to preservice employment. Jack "took thirty of those forty days to look around for work on the West Coast." One talent agent offered him a commercial announcer position on the CBS Orson Welles show. Jack asked the salary and remembers the response: "This is an opportunity to build your name and reputation; it pays $75." He countered, "Orson Welles is a genius in the history of entertainment. He has ten times the talent I have—but no more than that. I know he's getting $2,500, so I want $250, one-tenth."

They did not reach an agreement. In the meantime, another agent asked if he would be willing to change his surname, "because a name like Brickhouse would detract from the stars of a show." He responded, "My idea of a career is not anonymity," and says he never regretted the decision to keep his family name.

Nor did he regret another decision made while still in California. From Chicago, WGN's Frank Schreiber, "really my patron saint in the business, telephoned to ask whether I was returning to the station. I said that if I did I wanted a broadcasting assignment at the Republican and Democratic national political conventions, both to be held in Chicago that summer. Schreiber thought it over for a minute and agreed. He knew I was a pretty good special events man, which is often true for sports announcers."

Jack returned to Chicago, the second-largest radio market in the nation, in January 1944. He spent much of his free time that spring preparing for the conventions. Nelda helped him learn about the candidates, the delegates, the party platforms. "I really worked. I knew more about most of those men than maybe even their mothers knew about them."

Instead of broadcasting the 1944 baseball season, WGN chose the Mutual network schedule of soap operas, theater, and children's programs, so when Jack got back from service "there were no games for me to do." In May he broadcast the Illinois Republican state convention from Springfield. That summer he covered the national Republican and Democratic conventions from Chicago Stadium, both for WGN and the Mutual Broadcasting System. By then the largest national network, Mutual assigned a staff of fifteen newsmen and commentators, with Jack as the anchor broadcaster.

At the Republican convention in June, presidential candidate Thomas Dewey and his choice for vice president, John W. Bricker, were nominated on the first ballot. Mutual had also scheduled the session on adopting the party platform, recalls Jack, "canceling some of the kid shows if necessary." He explains:

> The other networks did not plan to cover the platform session. All well and good, except that it was delayed for nearly an hour after the chairman, Ohio

senator Robert Taft, became lost between the head-
quarters Stevens Hotel [now the Chicago Hilton and
Towers] and Chicago Stadium. We had to take it
away at 4:00—boom. How would we hold an audience until Taft arrived? That's where all our preparation paid off.

I called it like a baseball game: "I see Harold
Rainville down there talking to Thomas Dewey's
man. Harold, of course, is the executive assistant to
Everett Dirksen. We know Dewey favored Dirksen as
a vice presidential possibility," and so on and so
forth. "We'll find out what they're talking about." We
filled those fifty-five minutes easily.

A month later Jack reported from the Democratic
national convention, which quickly became more exciting
than the Republican gathering had been. On the second day
of the proceedings—just a few weeks after the Allied invasion of Normandy—WGN staff received the stunning news
bulletin of an assassination attempt against Adolf Hitler by
some of his own officers. Jack was escorted to the podium
in Chicago Stadium to report the bulletin to the several thousand delegates.

Roosevelt, unopposed for a historic fourth presidential
nomination, wanted to replace Henry A. Wallace as his running mate. Jack reported to his radio listeners on the maneuverings that led to the choice of Senator Harry S Truman
from Missouri. "What fascinated me was how the Andy
Frain usher organization jockeyed the Wallace people," who
planned to pack the convention for a major rally.

Chicago Mayor Edward J. Kelly "came up with a favorite
son nomination for United States senator Scott Lucas, from
Havana, Illinois," who had also been nominated at the 1940

convention. "Kelly advised Andy Frain of what was going on, so he managed to split the seating arrangements for Wallace delegates. Frain divided and conquered those supporters," and Lucas played the favorite son (later revealing, "Candidly, I was not a serious candidate"). The *New York Times* referred to the maneuver as the "second Missouri Compromise"; Kelly termed it "good politics."

During a lull in the proceedings Jack had the opportunity for an interview with James Farley, the postmaster general. Several years earlier in Peoria, Farley had been at the Pere Marquette Hotel after dedicating a post office in nearby Galesburg.

There was a special presidential suite at the Pere Marquette, where WMBD had a permanent line to interview celebrities. I went over there about 10:00 at night to get an OK to interview him the next morning. I opened the door to what I thought was the reception room of his suite, but it was the bedroom. There was the postmaster general of the United States of America in his undershorts—that's all he had on—stuffing his wallet between the double mattresses on the bed!

He heard me come in and wondered if he was being robbed, and I was terrified at seeing the postmaster general in that situation. It didn't take him long to size me up, and then I managed to blurt out why I was there. He laughed a little and then said, "Sure." The next morning we had a very good interview. I got a wonderful letter from him after he got back to Washington, which meant a great deal to this young man.

In 1944 Roosevelt and Farley parted company on the third-term issue, but Farley was still a powerhouse at the convention. And he lived in New York at the Waldorf Hotel. When the Cubs were in town, we stayed there, and Farley would visit us in the lobby. Herbert Hoover had an apartment in the Waldorf Towers, and Farley said that every once in a while Hoover would call him to come up and visit. I thought it would have been great to sit and listen to a conversation between those two old pros.

Jack's coverage of both 1944 conventions received notice in national publications, with *Billboard* magazine reporting that he "did one of the top radio jobs. . . . Using the Midwestern approaches all the way, Brickhouse managed to keep his work simple and understandable." *Variety* concurred that Mutual had "a well-synchronized" team, with Jack as the principal announcer. In a Peoria newspaper, Gomer Bath wrote about his former WMBD colleague, "Our idea of versatility is for an announcer to be able to jump from a baseball broadcast or a boxing bout into the political atmosphere of a state or national convention and get by with it."

Later in the year Jack and ABC broadcaster Harry Wismer were named as announcers for the All-Star Football Game between the college All-Stars and the national champion Chicago Bears. With many of their regular players and their coach George Halas away in the service, the Bears managed to slip by the All-Stars, 24–21. Over the years Jack would have the national broadcasting assignments for another dozen All-Star Football Games.

For the twenty-nine-year-old broadcaster, 1945 was an eventful year. In January he was in Washington, D.C., covering the Roosevelt inauguration on Mutual. "My picture was taken at the White House as I broadcast his last inaugural. Back in Chicago I asked Mayor Ed Kelly if he would have the president autograph my memento. Kelly agreed but said to be patient. He knew, though the public didn't, that Roosevelt was on the high seas for the Yalta Conference with Stalin and Churchill."

Three months later, on April 12, Brickhouse was at the WGN studio preparing for the evening news broadcast when disk jockey Lee Bennett received a telephone bulletin that Roosevelt had died. Bennett refused to air the unconfirmed story, so Jack spoke with a station writer, Howard Earl. Assured that the message was not a hoax, Jack looked at the quickly gathered staff, "who had heard the news through a mysterious grapevine. I stared at them and ad-libbed that awesome bulletin, 'President Franklin D. Roosevelt a few minutes ago died.' I was having trouble believing my own words. Of all the times I've addressed an open microphone, that was the most difficult and tragic assignment."

Jack had not broadcast major-league baseball during 1944, but he took leave from WGN in 1945 to freelance for WJJD, which was carrying the White Sox home games that season. His weekly salary was $350, plus $50 for broadcasting dugout interviews and another $50 for fifteen-minute sports programs. Also for WJJD he broadcast from the downtown Oriental Theater another version of "Man on the Street." Then just before the end of the baseball season, Elson returned from the navy. "Because he had seniority with the sponsor," he replaced Brickhouse as the Sox announcer.

Still associated with WGN as well, Jack hosted the "Country Sheriff" comedy series and the "Answer Man" show, responding to inquiries from listeners. One often-asked question and his answer: "Is Chicago really the windiest city?" "No, Buffalo, New York, has that distinction. Chicago is the twentieth-windiest city. And by the way, its nickname came not from the weather but from its 'windy' politicians."

Toward the end of the war Jack participated in a lighthearted salute to an unlikely hero—"Siwash, the beer drinking duck":

A young Illinois Marine, Francis Fagan, on liberty in the South Seas, won a duck in a sideshow raffle. He and his pals decided to adopt the duck as their mascot, and they named her Siwash. They taught her to drink beer, and she loved it, got to the point where she demanded it.

During some big Pacific invasions, there was Siwash, plowing along in the water, "quack, quack," right alongside the Marines. She got nipped by a bullet, and the guys gave her the Purple Heart. She made headlines in the United States and was invited to join a war bonds tour.

When Fagan brought Siwash home, Chicago civic leaders decided to hold a tribute to her. Where else? At the Drake Hotel. The idea caught the fancy of the city. Mayor Kelly and several other dignitaries came to the luncheon. The master of ceremonies was Nathaniel Leverone, chairman of Canteen Corporation and a popular toastmaster.

Siwash sat in the place of honor at the head table, in a baby's high chair, with a napkin tied around her neck. She did justice to the food and kept up a loud conversation during the entire luncheon. WGN broadcast the program, and Brickhouse was assigned as the announcer. I never had a more enjoyable assignment. Lincoln Park Zoo offered her a home; Purina offered a lifetime supply of food. It was a marvelous demonstration of good humor that Americans, and particularly Chicagoans, can produce when the occasion warrants.

In the mid-1940s, a *Fortune* magazine survey indicated that radio listening had become "more popular among men and women than any other form of recreation" and that they "spent more time listening to radio than on any other activity outside of working and sleeping." Also during those years, according to historian David Halberstam, major-league baseball "mesmerized the American people as it never had before and never would again. Baseball, more than almost anything else, seemed to symbolize normalcy and a return to life in America as it had been before Pearl Harbor."

In that environment Jack, "at liberty" after the 1945 White Sox season, sought a new broadcasting position. Traveling to New York, he auditioned for the Yankees—but Russ Hodges was hired, to work with lead announcer Mel Allen. "It turned out to be a break for me," relates Jack, "because then I got the number-one job with the New York Giants." According to the *Chicago Tribune*, he negotiated a salary of $35,000 for broadcasting the 1946 Giants season.

In the months prior to his departure from Chicago, Jack continued with WGN assignments and numerous personal appearances. As speaker at the LaSalle-Peru Elks lodge, his comments to the more than two hundred attendees were reported in the local newspaper. He predicted that Mexico would become "a big baseball country" and thought that

African-American players could have a significant role in the major leagues: "For instance, the impact of the signing of Jackie Robinson by Brooklyn is hard to see as yet. Major-league club owners apparently don't feel the proportion of Negro stars to others will cause any great inroads, while Negro pro leagues have been on the uprise and promoters are reluctant to see their players go with the majors for fear of losing their stars."

Giving his perspective on sports announcing, Jack said that baseball fans were the most ardent sports followers: "In a football game you can call Jones scoring a touchdown when Smith made the score, and nobody but the boy's father usually writes you. That's not baseball. Just try saying 'Hack doubles hard to left, driving in a run—and let's see now—that makes 68 for the season!' The next day two hundred letters come in; all of them tell 'you jerk, you bum, that was 69—why don't you go back to Peoria!' "

In New York, Jack prepared for his role as the Giants' broadcaster on independent radio station WMCA. The team had finished fifth in 1944 and 1945, but the owners were predicting a winning season in 1946. Among their leading players were Bill Rigney, Whitey Lockman, Buddy Blattner, Johnny Mize, and newly acquired Walker Cooper. What the owners did not anticipate was losing star pitcher Sal Maglie and eight other players—the most in the majors—to higher salaries in the fast-growing Mexican League.

From the beginning Jack encountered problems in New York:

WMCA had a deal with a prominent New York newspaper to do five minutes of news every hour on the hour. Even with the baseball games the paper insisted

that the station still carry the news. I said, "You can't
do that; you can't interrupt the game." But they said,
"Those are your orders." Sure enough, we couldn't
have set the stage any better. The Giants had the
bases loaded with all-time hero and manager Mel Ott
at bat, and they took it away from me to do five minutes of news. Of course the switchboard lit up immediately. Then the paper agreed to cancel the news
series.

WMCA was owned by a well-meaning gentleman
named Nathan Straus of the family that owned a
chain of retail stores. He knew nothing about baseball and was an idealistic man. Someone filled him in
on baseball terminology, and once he sent this memo
to his general manager: "Mr. Stark, I wish you would
speak to the operators of the baseball teams and
impress upon them the importance of completing
their games in the prescribed number of innings.
Lately they have used additional innings, which I have
to consider almost a deliberate attempt to disrupt
our programming schedule"!

Jack's broadcasting assistant and commentator with the
Giants was WMCA's young sports director, Steve Ellis.

Ellis was the only guy I ever worked with who
became a problem. He had never done one inning,
not one inning, of professional baseball, major or
minor. I said to him, "Steve, this is my living; you got
your job through clout. But if you will listen to me,
I will teach you as much as I can about baseball." I
admit that I was doing it for my own protection,

because a chain is as strong as its weakest link. Nobody was going to say, "That Brickhouse is a lousy broadcaster" or "Steve Ellis is a lousy broadcaster." They'd say, "Those two guys are lousy!"—especially with that ball club, which turned out to be a loser. And Brickhouse/Ellis was not a good broadcasting team.

Jack looked forward to the Giants' first game against the Dodgers, "one of the great baseball rivalries."

I sat on the Ebbets Field bench with Leo Durocher, the Dodgers manager. I told him I knew about some of the interesting and eccentric Dodgers fans, then asked him, "Have you ever had one stop you cold with his or her remarks?"

Leo said, "Just once, a few years ago. We were playing the Phillies, and both ball clubs were pounding each other. Four runs behind in the fifth inning, we filled the bases. I sent in pinch hitter Babe Phelps, who was slowed up by then but could still hit the ball. He came in with a pinch grand slam and tied the game for us. Neither team's pitching was any good, and in the eighth inning we were four runs behind again. As I was looking at the bench, from the box seats I heard, "Yeah, Durocher, you bum! Why'd you use up Phelps in the fifth inning? Now's when you need him!"

After the Giants and Dodgers split one midseason doubleheader, Dodgers broadcaster Red Barber needled Durocher about the game they had lost. Getting a testy

response, Barber then asked him to try being "a nice guy—
for a change." Durocher pointed to the Giants bench and singled out the great Mel Ott. "Look over there. Do you know
a nicer guy than Mel Ott? Or any of the other Giants? Why,
they're the nicest guys in the world. And where are they? In
last place!" His remarks were printed in the *New York Jour-
nal-American*, condensed to "Nice guys finish last." The
nice-guy Giants did finish, in Jack's words, "a bad last, eighth
out of eight."

While in New York, Jack also was hired by Paramount
News for voice-overs on movie newsreels. Twice a week he
narrated news and sports events, "great national exposure"
in Paramount's forty-five hundred theaters. Some of his free
days and evenings were spent in Manhattan restaurants and
bars. At Toots Schor's restaurant, he mingled with entertainment and sports celebrities and became friends with
Harry Caray, in his second year as broadcaster for the St.
Louis Cardinals. Jack recalls that he and Caray "closed Toots
Schor's more than once." Nelda Brickhouse joined her husband in September, but both were anxious to return to their
Chicago home for the off-season. WGN assignments awaited,
including a return to Big Ten football, which Jack had last
broadcast in 1943.

Early in 1947 the Giants replaced the inexperienced
broadcaster Ellis with Frank Frisch, a former star infielder
who had been fired as manager of the Pittsburgh Pirates after
the 1946 season. Jack looked forward to working with the
Hall of Famer until he learned by telephone in Chicago that,
because of Frisch's higher salary, his own promised pay
increase was being canceled. "As a matter of fact," he was
told, "we may have to cut you a little bit." An angry Jack

resigned over the phone. "I wasn't fired, but I didn't go back. It turned out to be the best move I ever made."

Remaining in Chicago, Jack decided to "find out what television was like. Anybody who could see beyond his nose knew that it would be important someday." He was hired by WBKB, "the only television station in town, at the modest price of $30 per game," for the 1947 Cubs season. His partner on the experimental series was a television pioneer, Joe Wilson, later nicknamed "Whispering Joe" from his broadcasts of bowling tournaments. WBKB, Channel 4, which had begun broadcasting in 1943, was owned by John Balaban, who years earlier had been a film salesman for Jack's father.

According to Curt Smith in *Voices of the Game*, the Cubs' owner and managers intuitively felt "that television would make fans of viewers and, eventually, patrons of fans." Jack concurred with Smith: "Like . . . [William Wrigley, Phil Wrigley's] dad, who'd recognized, early on, what radio could do as a promotional tool, Phil Wrigley did the same in television. . . . It made fans. Other owners refused to let home games be televised—they thought it would cut down on attendance."

One special event in 1947 is unforgettable to Jack—his broadcast of an appearance by Babe Ruth. Visiting a number of cities on behalf of the American Legion Junior Babe Ruth Baseball program, the legendary star arrived in Chicago a day prior to the Comiskey Park ceremony. The *Sun* reported Mayor Martin Kennelly's praise of Ruth as "the greatest man ever connected with sports," who impressed "upon the nation's youth the benefit of clean living and clean sports." Ruth responded, "I love these kids. . . . The Legion baseball leagues have got them away from the pool halls and taught them the value of clean sports." (Earlier in his career, as Jack reminds, "Babe was one of baseball's greatest playboys.")

On August 16, 1947—a year to the day before he died— the fifty-two-year-old Ruth was honored in a ceremony prior to the junior baseball game. More than thirteen thousand children and parents gave him tremendous ovations as the motorcade entered the stadium and again as he greeted the fans. Jack remembers the day:

> Ruth was, and even is now, the greatest single figure the game of baseball has ever known. At Comiskey Park that day, he was to address the kids. He had throat cancer. Everybody knew it; he had a hoarse voice. We wanted to tape his address, because maybe it would be his last appearance in Chicago—which it was. We were told, however, that if he saw a radio microphone and knew there was a broadcast going on in addition to the public address mike for the kids, it might bother him. So the WGN engineer masked the call letters on the side of his box when we went into the park, and he hid under the stands. The taping microphone was attached to the PA mike, so there was no indication of a broadcast, just a spare mike.
>
> I introduced Ruth, and there was something about the whole spirit that caught him right in the heart. All of a sudden he realized, at this place and

time in his life, what these kids meant to him. He broke down. His address was one of the most dramatic I've ever heard.

After the program Ruth and his wife and daughter were escorted to the stands, where they watched the American Legion contest. According to the *Tribune*, Ruth followed "every play in the game—and he autografed [sic] every baseball brought to him in his box near home plate." To Jack, "That event was a great experience; I was very proud to be part of it."

In the fall of 1947 Jack was named broadcaster for the Chicago Cardinals football team, expected to be a championship contender. At preseason practice coach Jim Conzelman announced to a *Daily News* reporter: "This is the finest-looking bunch of players *anybody* has *ever* seen in a Cardinal camp!"

The Cardinals' Charlie Trippi, an All-Star in college, made a play that remains vivid to Jack. "The touchdown run I remember most was one that was called back," a punt return by Trippi against the Washington Redskins. "Charlie wasn't fast, so every Redskin had at least one shot at him. Some had two, some three. The play was called back because officials charged that Cardinals end Mal Kutner had roughed the punter. Do you want to know what Mal did? He roughed the punter's foot with his lips. They had to take six stitches in Kutner's mouth because he was so rough."

The Cardinals and Chicago Bears played the final game of the season tied for first place. The Cardinals' 30–21 win clinched the Western Division crown. With the "dream back-field" of Trippi, Paul Christman, Elmer Angsman, Babe Dimancheff, and Pat Harder and defensive backs Marshall Goldberg and Bill De Correvont, they went on to the championship game against the Philadelphia Eagles. Jack announced the game from Comiskey Park, simulcast on television and radio. Trippi scored on a seventy-five-yard run, "the most spectacular run" of the longest season in NFL history. "He had another for a fifty-yard touchdown, and Angsman had two seventy-yard touchdown runs." The Cardinals' 28–21 win brought their first championship since 1925—and at this writing never again repeated, either in Chicago or later, after the team moved to St. Louis and then on to Phoenix, Arizona.

CHAPTER 4

On Television

As one of chicago's star broadcasters, Brick-house hosted the first television show from the downtown Merchandise Mart in January 1948. He opened the live two-hour WBKB telecast by interviewing Mart owner Joseph P. Kennedy, the former ambassador to Great Britain and father of future president John F. Kennedy. Then, as reported in the Mart newsletter, Brickhouse and the *Chicago Sun*'s Virginia Marmaduke "raced from floor to floor, showroom to showroom," describing to an estimated eleven thousand television viewers "the latest in electric blankets" and other electronics, housewares, and furniture.

Of all the new products available to postwar consumers, by far the most popular was the television set. By 1948 thirty thousand employees of the Chicago companies Zenith, Motorola, and Admiral manufactured nearly half of the sets made in the United States. WGN was one of eighteen stations nationwide that entered the television era that year, and from the beginning Jack was a principal figure at WGN-TV.

In February he rejoined the station as sports service manager and broadcaster. His first official television assignment came on March 5, covering the International Golden Gloves tournament. He was the announcer on that first WGN telecast, a test transmission from Chicago Stadium. "We weren't really aware of the history but were just wondering whether we would have much of an audience," Jack says, and recalls the guests he interviewed between bouts. "One was Will Harridge, president of the American League; another was Arch Ward, sports editor of the *Tribune*, who originated the Golden Gloves. The third was Ezzard Charles, a light heavyweight in those days."

The *Tribune*'s Larry Wolters reported on the "varied reception" of that first telecast:

> The family and a few friends had gathered about the television receiver to watch WGN-TV do its first scheduled telecast—the Golden Gloves finals. The test pattern came in fine. But when the engineers switched to Chicago Stadium, we got only the pictures—not Jack Brickhouse's voice. No amount of tinkering with knobs would bring in the sound.
>
> We hurried over to a neighbor's house. They were getting good pictures (on a different-brand set) and also the excellent commentary of Brickhouse. Next we called on another neighbor, who has a set exactly like ours. He was getting swell pictures. Also Mr. B.
>
> Our experience wasn't unusual. WGN-TV engineers got more than three hundred calls from television set owners that evening. Many calls came in congratulating the station on the excellence of the pictures and sound. Among these was one from a viewer in Crystal Lake, 47 miles out, who reported good reception, and another from a looker at Kewanee, 140 miles away, who got faint reception. (He shouldn't have expected anything at all at that distance!)

Many callers complained that they weren't getting any sound but were getting pictures and vice versa. Others got nothing. . . . All who called were advised that their receivers and antennas might require adjustments by servicemen before they could expect to receive WGN-TV signals clearly. Many expressed complete surprise that such measures are indicated when a new station comes on the air.

After the experimental WBKB-TV baseball series in 1947, Cubs owner Philip K. Wrigley decided to continue televising the ball games at Wrigley Field, as his father two decades earlier had decided on radio. According to Jack, "The broadcasts built loyalty and stirred interest. Wrigley's thinking in '48 was that the guy who became a Cubs fan as a result of television would sooner or later come out to Wrigley Field."

In April, WGN-TV announced an arrangement for televising all home games of both the Cubs and the White Sox, with Jack as the announcer. Wrigley's statement on the plan was reported in the *Tribune*:

> As pioneers in the televising of baseball games as they were in the radio broadcasting of baseball, the Chicago Cubs are happy to have WGN-TV telecasting the Cubs home games from Wrigley Field this year.
>
> The Cubs are gratified that the televising of baseball games . . . is not meeting with the resistance that greeted the pioneer efforts in radio broadcasting we inaugurated in 1925.
>
> For many years there was a suspicion among baseball people that broadcasting would hurt attendance at ball games. Now, of course, everyone recognizes that radio broadcasting has been a potent factor in stimulating baseball attendance.

> We are confident that television, handled with imagination and understanding, will bring baseball closer to vast numbers of Americans, and will result eventually in bringing many more persons to ball parks, to get a closeup, personal view of the dramatic scenes and colorful characters they become acquainted with on the television screens.

Baseball coverage began with the preseason Cubs–White Sox exhibition series. Adaptations at Wrigley Field in preparation for the video coverage were described in the *Tribune*:

> On either side of the Cubs' dugout, television cameras will work at ground levels. The wall, four feet on each side, has been removed the width of three box seats to provide television holes. In these recesses, the camera men will operate. WGN-TV will be on the right dugout, WBKB on the left.
>
> Television cameras will be all over the field— on the left field wall out of the playing field, in the football press box, and on the ramp extending from the press box back of home plate.

Jack recalled that the camera crew "worked out on a couple of high school games just to get the feel of things before tackling that first major-league game." He telecast the city series with WGN associate Harry Creighton, and they continued as partners in the WGN television booth for nearly ten years.

Once the 1948 regular season was under way, Jack described to the *Tribune* his perceptions of the new medium:

> For the next few years, at least, sports coverage will be far and away the most important single element in television programming. It's a safe

bet that up to 50 per cent of television hours, both live shows and films, will be in the field of athletics. . . .

Fortunately co-incident, as far as sports boosters are concerned, is the fact that television today lacks facilities and man power to produce more than a few studio shows daily. All the resources of Hollywood, radio, television, and the legitimate stage if pooled could present no more than a scant 4 or 5 hours daily.

Tho [sic] an infant, television (and its viewers) demands top-notch programs when available. What better place is there to find this quality than in the field of sports? The stages are built— Wrigley Field, Comiskey Park, Chicago Stadium. The "show" may be a red-hot pennant fight or the blazing finish of a football championship race.

In *Voices of the Game*, Curt Smith summarized the 1948 Chicago baseball season: "Without knowing it, in that remote, infantile year, like Donner harnessing the Pass, Brickhouse began a continuum—an intimacy between ball club and viewer—that decades later, in the wake of cable and, thus, WGN's intrusion into millions of American households, fostered for the Cubs an enormous national sect."

In August of 1948 Jack was at Soldier Field for the first televised All-Star Football Game. A sellout crowd of more than a hundred thousand watched the champion Chicago Cardinals defeat the College All-Stars, 28–0. And according to the *Tribune*, the television coverage attracted a half-million viewers:

. . . all over the city and suburbs, radio, appliance, and furniture stores put sets in the windows. And the crowds that gathered on the sidewalks forced

passing pedestrians to detour to the streets. In
Chicago the tavern reaction was the same as in
the suburbs—television brought many, many customers. John Casey, owner of the tavern at 8724
Cottage Grove av., estimated the business increase
at 100 per cent. So did Roy Glick, owner of the
establishment at 1652 E. 52d st. It was pointed out
that football lends itself admirably to television,
and that the game did a good job of interesting
the general public in the new entertainment
medium.

In October, Jack again demonstrated versatility, with a
two-hour Chicago Stadium telecast of the Roy Rogers World
Championship Rodeo. Viewers were entertained by the King
of the Cowboys, Dale Evans, and the horse Trigger, along
with demonstrations of calf roping, steer wrestling, and
bull riding. In sports Jack covered a schedule of Catholic
high school football games—the first televised high school
league series in the country, according to the *Tribune*, and
an eight-game college football schedule, including remotes
from Northwestern, Notre Dame, and the University of
Illinois.

Continuing WGN radio broadcasts as well, he won a first-
place Chicago Federated Advertising Club award for his
"Spotlight on Sports." The *Tribune*'s popular "Harold Teen"
comic strip was expanded to radio: the collegiate Teen
became a disk jockey, and the war-era Jackson Brickhouse
was replaced by another character based on the real Brickhouse. According to Jack, the "Harold Teen" creator, Carl
Ed, was sometimes assisted in writing the strip by his son-
in-law, Fred Reynolds, a WGN employee and one of Jack's
golfing partners.

Reynolds created an eccentric character in the strip and named him Brick Jackhouse. The first episode showed me, Jackhouse, on the golf course—Fred always said I had a weird swing anyway—swinging at the ball. I missed the ball three times, picked it up, walked off, and said, "This course is too tough for me." Well, Fred got a laugh out of it. This much you have to know about cartoonists: if they get a laugh with something, they milk it forever. Then he had me opening a dress shop, wearing a lace handkerchief in my sleeve. Damn near ran me out of the country.

Northwestern University students played the cartoon characters on the new radio show. According to the *Tribune*, Brick gave listeners "the latest gossip from his fictional fashion emporium, the Maison de Jackhouse."

During the late 1940s and into the 1950s, Jack hosted a popular weekly radio program called "Marriage License Romances." From the Chicago City Hall he interviewed couples applying for their marriage licenses.

We used the office of the Cook County clerk, a man named Mike Flynn. When he left in 1950, a young fellow by the name of Richard J. Daley became county clerk. That's how he and I became acquainted; he let us continue the program.

Over the course of the series, I interviewed hundreds of couples. One time I was at a bar at the Phoenix airport, waiting for a plane bringing in the bandleader Eddie Howard. We were staying at the same place and were going to play golf together. The bartender was not very friendly, and before long he

was downright surly. It turned out that I had interviewed him on "Marriage License Romances" back
in Chicago, and the marriage went sour. He identified me with a very bad situation, so he just couldn't
let himself be nice to me.

But every once in a while, even today, I run into
grandparents who were on the show and whose marriages did work out.

By the late 1940s television accounted for the single most
significant change in the use of leisure time—and as predicted
sports programs led both national and local schedules. In
those years Chicago hosted the two major-league baseball
teams, professional hockey, football, and basketball, along
with a regular schedule of boxing and wrestling events.

In 1949 Jack and Harry Creighton began broadcasting
both Cubs and Sox games on WGN-TV. "Jack and I had the
greatest job in town," Creighton told a reporter years later.
"We only covered home games, so we never had to travel.
And we were watching baseball. Doesn't that sound great?"
Creighton left WGN in 1957, but Jack continued with both
teams for eighteen years.

Jack's great memory of the April 19, 1949, Cubs season
opener was not of the game but of the birth of his only child,
Jeanne. "I don't remember a thing about the game—except
I think the Pirates won," Brickhouse recalled with a grin.
Another daughter had died at birth two years earlier.

In May the *Tribune* named six "Leading Entertainers in
the Field of Television": Fran Allison, "the only live cast
member" of the "Kukla, Fran, & Ollie" show; hostess Jinx
Falkenburg; Arthur Godfrey; Milton Berle, "zaniest video
comic of them all"; Gertrude Berg as Molly Goldberg of

"The Goldbergs"; and Jack Brickhouse, "Chicago's ace television sportscaster."

WGN-TV joined the DuMont network in 1949, and Jack received a major career boost when DuMont selected him for the 1950 All-Star Baseball Game. Alone in the tiny Comiskey Park broadcast booth with "an inexpensive set of headphones," he telecast the midseason classic, which in the previous four years had been won by the American League.

> That 1950 game was my first big break on network television. In the ninth inning, Ralph Kiner tied it for the Nationals with a homer. Red Schoendienst hit one in the fourteenth for a 4–3 win. To that time, it was the most thrilling All-Star game ever played.
>
> That was also the game in which Ted Williams, going after a fly ball, crashed into the wall. It was unfortunate that the trainer for the squad rubbed Ted's elbow a little while and said, "It'll be fine now, Ted." All it was was broken. And Ted was out for the year.
>
> But the interesting sidelight was that a guy named Billy Goodman took over Williams's job in left field and won the batting title that year. There actually was some conjecture as to whether Williams could get his job back—Ted Williams, the greatest hitter that some of us have ever seen.

Jack's broadcast of the game brought him national recognition. According to the *Tribune*'s Wolters:

> The televiewing public got the kind of break it deserved the other day when Jack Brickhouse was chosen to do the commentary for the All-Star

baseball game. Baseball and Brickhouse go together—they're a natural combination on TV, and
they never showed to any better advantage than
during those 14 innings last Tuesday when the
bluebloods of the major leagues battled it out.

If you didn't get a seat in Comiskey Park,
you did just about as well watching WGN-TV (or
any of 35 other stations tied in for this classic)
and following Brickhouse's expert and informed
comment.

Also in 1950, Jack began a writing project for publica-
tion, the annual *Jack Brickhouse's Major League Record
Book*.

The official statistician for the National League was
the Elias News Bureau in New York. Every year they
would print a record book, adding maybe a dozen or
two new records. They would send the book to the
ball clubs and to the reporters, but it wasn't available
for public sale. I asked, "Send me one; I'm a reporter." Sometimes they did; sometimes they didn't.
I got a little upset with them. Then I thought, Those
records are public domain; I'll put out my own book.

I got the official statistician for the American
League, John Phillips, who was with the Howe
Bureau in Chicago. He painstakingly went through
every record in the Elias book and found mistakes.
He got the correct answers—box scores and all.

I sold enough ads for our book to pay for it and
to help buy a new car every year. Phillips and I put
out the book for twenty-one years, but then my

schedule was such that I didn't have time to be on the phone, hustling ads. Still, about three or four times a year at the ballpark some fan will come up with a copy and ask me to autograph it.

During the summer of 1950 a proud Brickhouse took his fourteen-month-old daughter to her first baseball game. According to Nelda, Jeanne "became fascinated by Phil Cavarretta's cap, an early sign" to her mother that she would become a sports fan. Nelda, too, was the subject of celebrity attention. In a *Tribune* article titled "What It's Like to Be Wife of TV Sportscaster," she was depicted as a busy entertainer of "friends from the sports world." According to the reporter, she helped answer fan mail and prepare broadcasting scripts. "But the phone can ring, research wait, and mail remain sealed if Brickhouse is on the radio or telecasting. . . . Mrs. Brickhouse and Jeannie never miss an opportunity to hear or see him, whether he is telecasting a football game or wrestling match, or airing sports scores."

During the summer of 1950 from Cog Hill Country Club in Lemont, Illinois, Jack narrated an all-star golf program—featuring Cary Middlecoff and Sam Snead—for distribution to local television stations. That pilot program, produced by Walter Schwimmer and Wilson Sporting Goods and later sold to ABC, has been credited as the impetus to the continuing popularity of televised golf. In August, Jack again broadcast the All-Star Football Game over WGN-TV and twenty-nine DuMont network stations nationwide, as the collegiate All-Stars defeated the Philadelphia Eagles at Soldier Field, 17–7. Recently Jack recalled an incident at that stadium:

When Colonel Robert R. McCormick ran the *Tri-bune*, he insisted that his reporters refer to the sta-dium as "Soldiers' Field, because it belongs to all soldiers." And we broadcasters always tried to honor his wishes, too.

Once, though, while we were telecasting an All-Star Football Game there, someone penetrated our defenses with a call purportedly from the colonel's office that we should say "Soldier Field." It turned out to be a hoax—probably some guy in a bar—but we made the change during the game. Fortunately, we didn't receive any memo from the colonel's twenty-fourth floor of the Tribune Tower.

In October, Jack, along with Mel Allen, Jim Britt, and Gene Kelly, were named to the World Series television broad-casting team. Jack credited his selection to his well-received coverage of the All-Star Baseball Game that summer. The Gillette Company was the exclusive radio and television spon-sor of the World Series. At the "Gillette Cavalcade of Sports" press conference prior to the New York–Philadelphia series, Jack responded to questions about his allegiance: "I don't see how I can possibly help but be neutral because my job out there in Chicago is to cover both leagues, and I don't have to worry about any heartaches after the Series is over."

The telecast of the first game at Philadelphia's Shibe Park attracted an estimated thirty million viewers as far west as Omaha, Nebraska, and Jack remembers that "our picture was lost for the first half hour!" In four low-scoring games, Casey Stengel's Yankees, with Joe DiMaggio, Gene Wood-ling, and Phil Rizzuto, swept the contest, capturing their sec-ond straight World Series.

In January 1951, *Look* magazine announced its first annual television awards: "Television graduated from growing pains to maturity in 1950. . . . Where once anything that flickered was good for an evening's rapt and silent attention, in 1950 it took consistently good programs to hold an audience. *Look* here salutes the best of those programs," among which was the "Gillette Cavalcade of Sports" World Series coverage.

From 1950 to 1951 the number of televisions in Chicago-area homes increased from an estimated 52,000 to 325,000, with the majority of households having at least one set. On WGN-TV, Jack hosted a daily series, "Chicago Calendar," moving "from his office desk each noon . . . to interview interesting personalities and subjects of the day, each in his own setting." On April 26, 1951, he broadcast the MacArthur Day Parade in downtown Chicago, honoring Korean War general Douglas MacArthur.

We had a broadcast setup for the parade on Michigan Avenue, all the way down to Soldier Field— where there was to be a MacArthur rally. It turned out to be a huge parade. They had me on a raised platform on Michigan Avenue in front of WGN and Tribune Tower, with our television cameras. Then I ran down to Soldier Field and broadcast from there.

The night before I had gone to Mayor Martin Kennelly's office, where they were making the preparations. I said that we were going to broadcast from near Tribune Tower and asked if Kennelly would make sure the parade didn't go too fast so we would have a little time with our cameras and microphones.

When that limousine with Kennelly and Mac-

Arthur got to Tribune Tower, the whole parade stopped for about five minutes. It really piled up there; we almost ran out of things to talk about. Did he cooperate!

In the early 1950s Jack was approached to telecast Boys Major League Baseball, an organization formed by his friend Mel Thillens.

Mel had pulled out of Little League because of the restriction that he could recruit only from a certain neighborhood. Mel owned Thillens Stadium at Devon and Kedzie, a very fine stadium. "If some kid from the south side of Chicago wants to play in my ball-park, what's wrong with that?" So he made up his own league, and a sponsor picked it up, and WGN tele-vised the games.

We had a lot of fun out there. Most kids can run; most kids can catch a ball. But I was amazed at some of those arms, the way they could throw the ball. Every once in a while today I'll run into a business-man or doctor or lawyer who'll say, "The first time I knew about you, you televised my team in Thillens's little league."

The league included some five hundred nine- to twelve-year-olds, and Jack's weekly play-by-play garnered praise from a New York sports columnist, Jerry Mitchell: "Jack Brickhouse, the likeable giant who used to broadcast the Giants' games here, has added to his television reputation with his introduction of the Little League games in the Chicago area. . . . Brickhouse, [teamed with] Don Cook, Dick

Lisendahl and Ernie Simon, earned the trade's plaudits by not sportscasting the youngsters' games just for laughs. . . . The games, broadcast on a national scale, were caught one night by an appreciative group of major league players."

Brickhouse credits Thillens's games with initiating a now-common view of televised baseball:

> In those days at the ballparks the theory was that all cameras were in just about the same direction—a camera behind the plate, one at third, one at first—instead of putting them in different places and jumping your audience all around. However, one night at Thillens Stadium, one of our cameramen said, "You know, Jack, that center field fence is only about a couple of hundred feet from the plate. If we could put a camera out there, I'll bet we'd get a nice shot of the catcher and the batter—see their eyes." I said that it sounded great to me. We got the OK from the director—a beautiful shot, the little pitcher, batter, catcher, umpire.
>
> It was so good that the next week we decided to experiment with it at Wrigley Field. Fortunately, the perspective at Wrigley Field is perfect from center field, just the proper height, the proper distance, so when you take that shot it looks like sixty feet, six inches—which it is. That same shot at some of the other ballparks would have it looking like the pitcher and catcher are shaking hands or so far apart that they don't even speak. But this was lucky, just plain lucky.
>
> On the air I said, "Our theory had always been to keep our cameras pointed in the same general

direction, but this particular shot also gives a good picture. Would you like for us to keep it in as well?" We got a thousand pieces of mail. All but about ten said "good picture," so we added it.

A very short time later NBC put in that shot on its "Game of the Week." NBC claimed to have originated it. Well, maybe it was an idea whose time had come, but I'm telling you, that shot was original with us—with Mel Thillens's "Boys Major League Baseball."

In the summer of 1951 Jack was again selected to telecast the All-Star Baseball Game, held in Detroit to commemorate the city's 250th anniversary. In his introductory remarks Jack reminisced about Briggs Stadium history:

A real baseball palace it is—a palace with quite a legend involving some of the real kings of the baseball world. This is where Ty Cobb did so many things for so many years, they'll be talked about in reverent tones so long as baseball lives. . . .

It's the park where they've never known a last-place team—and the only park in the majors able to make that statement. Detroit has had thirty first-division teams in the fifty years of the American League, winning seven pennants—the last in 1945 when they went on to whip the Cubs in the World Series, 4 out of 7.

Home runs paced the Nationals to an 8–3 win, but American League homers by Detroit's Vic Wertz and George Kell cheered the local fans.

The following month Jack again televised the All-Star Football Game, watching the five-time champion Cleveland Browns dominate the college players, 33–0. Arch Ward, the *Chicago Tribune* sports editor who originated the contest in 1934, wrote that the game "was carried to the largest audience in sports history. . . . A total of 520 Mutual Broadcasting system stations, and broadcasts to overseas service men, east and west, as well as TV pictures through 46 channels, made the evening's coverage the most thoro [sic] ever. . . . Jack Brickhouse and Harry Creighton worked a grand job on TV." (Ward was one of Jack's "heroes—my big brother." And Jack was an honorary pallbearer at Ward's funeral in 1955.)

In October, *The Sporting News* announced an annual video awards program "in keeping with the growing importance of television's role in baseball." The first-year honors went to Brickhouse, "TV commentator for White Sox (A.L.) games, and Russ Hodges of the Giants (N.L.)." *The Sporting News* described Jack as the busiest sports announcer on television, broadcasting "more baseball games than any other sportscaster . . . handling two major league clubs." Interviewed for *Baseball Magazine* regarding the award, Jack singled out his World Series and All-Star Game assignments "as the top events in sports that a person can be privileged to broadcast."

Two months later he received a *Look* magazine television award for the "Gillette Cavalcade of Sports" baseball coverage as the best sports program of 1951. Then that busiest year of his career was capped with a trip to Pasadena, California, for the 1952 New Year's Day Rose Bowl game between Stanford and the University of Illinois. Scheduled to telecast with Mel Allen, Jack lost their coin toss to decide the order for announcing. He broadcast the first half, "which turned out to be the better half." On the opening possession Illinois drove seventy-six yards to a touchdown, but after two closely played quarters, Stanford led 7–6. The second half was a rout, with Illinois winning 40–7.

Jack recalled in his published reminiscence *Thanks for Listening!*:

> In 1944, I was in the Marine Corps and stationed in San Diego. I had a couple days leave and hitch-hiked to Pasadena. I sat in the end zone in uniform and watched Southern Cal beat Washington, 29–0.
>
> It was eight years before I went to my second Rose Bowl game. I travelled a different route than I did in 1944. In 1952, I was broadcasting the game on national television and I was driven to the game in a limousine. . . . It was more fun to go to a bowl game as a paid broadcaster than it was as a Marine.

In spring of 1952 the Brickhouse family vacationed in St. Petersburg, Florida, prior to his joining the White Sox at spring training. During the year, in addition to Sox and Cubs home games, Jack telecast Thillens's little league games, some fifty wrestling matches, the Illinois-Iowa Big Ten basketball championship, Golden Gloves contests, and both the baseball and football All-Star Games. "For that All-Star Baseball Game, I traveled a round trip of nearly two thousand miles to describe three outs. Mel Allen and I were assigned to do the game, and we split the assignment. Mel took the first 4½ innings and then turned it over to me, with the Nationals ahead, 3–2. Bobby Shantz, the little American League left-hander, struck out Lockman, Robinson, and Musial. Then the rains came, and the game eventually was called. I had quite a trip just to describe three strikeouts."

That fall Jack and New York broadcaster Al Helfer had the radio assignment for the World Series, between the Dodgers and the Yankees. Mickey Mantle, a Yankee rookie in 1952, recalled in his autobiography *All My Octobers*:

> There was something special about a Subway Series, a rivalry that has all but vanished from the scene. When I was a rookie, remember, you had three teams in New York and two each in Chicago, Boston, St. Louis, and Philadelphia.
>
> Of course, we didn't take the subway. But the first day we boarded the team bus to take us to Ebbets Field, all the way out Second Avenue the fans were cheering and holding up signs of support. As soon as we crossed the bridge into Brooklyn, and turned onto Flatbush Avenue, it was like entering another world. The faces were flushed and contorted, the fans were screaming and cursing at us.
>
> . . . The 1952 World Series opened at Ebbets Field and, as great as they were, the Dodgers still had a quality of daffiness that dated back to leaner, losing times. You didn't know whether to feel sorry for the Dodgers or to view them as you would a dangerous, wounded animal. The team had blown the pennant on the last day of the two previous seasons.

The Dodgers boasted a power lineup—with Duke Snider, Jackie Robinson, and Gil Hodges—along with strong pitching. Yankees stars included Billy Martin, Gene Woodling, and Mantle. According to author Curt Smith, Helfer and Brickhouse "resounded over more than seven hundred stations" on the Mutual network, the Canadian Broadcasting Corporation, and the Armed Forces Radio Service.

To Jack the fifth and seventh games of the Series remain vivid.

> In the fifth inning of game five the Yankees touched Dodgers starter Carl Erskine for five runs. Dressen went out to talk to Erskine, then he bore down to retire every Yankee from then on—and Brooklyn won in eleven, 6–5!
>
> In game seven, I think everyone who was listening or watching remembers Billy Martin's lunging catch of Jackie Robinson's ball off the top of a blade of grass near the pitcher's mound—after first baseman Joe Collins lost the ball in the sun. This was in the seventh inning of the seventh game—and was one of the great clutch catches of all time. The Yankees were ahead 4–2, and the Dodgers had the bases filled with two out. Pee Wee Reese told me later that he could have scored from first base if Martin had missed the ball.

The Yankees won the game and thus their fourth consecutive championship. After the series columnist Jack Mabley wrote in the *Chicago Daily News*:

> The only way Chicago ever gets in the World Series in this generation is with Jack Brickhouse. . . . Jack is distinguished more for what he doesn't say than for what he does. In other cities an inning is a canto, stanza or a frame. In Chicago an inning is

called an inning. The bases are called first, second and third here. Our imaginative and somewhat boring neighbors prefer to cluck out initial hassock, keystone sack and hot corner. . . .

Brickhouse knows baseball and the men in it. He manages to a fair degree to keep his personal feelings out of his reporting. But what sets him apart from his brethren is the fact that using only plain, correct English, he conveys the excitement and color of the ball games effectively and pleasantly. He is indeed a rare bird, and we congratulate New York on being smart enough to hire him to do the series.

During the 1952 football season Jack provided radio coverage of Big Ten games and the Blue Gray Bowl, along with interview and commentary programs on both radio and television. For the second consecutive year he and Hodges shared the *Sporting News* national television awards.

In November, Jack traveled to his hometown as guest of the Peoria Sunday Morning Sports League. His appearance was described by *Journal* reporter Jack Rosenberg: "TV artist Jack Brickhouse—and the TV stands for 'terrific voice'—learned first-hand last night that his pride in Peoria is excelled only by Peoria's pride in him." Rosenberg presented the Brickhouse assessment of prominent baseball players:

Mickey Mantle (Yanks)—Potentially as great as Joe DiMaggio. Give him a couple of years. He has more speed than DiMag, too. I'd like to see the Cubs or White Sox buy him. . . . Warren Hacker (Cubs)—One of the greatest in the National league, unusual because he throws strikes. The average game now lasts from 2 hours, 20 minutes,

to four days. Hacker cuts 'em to 2 hours flat. . . .
Hank Sauer (Cubs)—He deserved the "most valuable award." Without him, the Cubs would have
finished in Joplin, Mo.

The 1953 sports season began for Jack on New Year's
Day, on CBS radio for the Orange Bowl game between the
Alabama Crimson Tide and Syracuse University. Played
before a record crowd, the game, he remembers, developed
"into a cross between a track meet and a basketball game."
Alabama "just killed Syracuse" 61–6, setting a scoring record
for a major bowl. Over the years Jack's college football
assignments would include several more Blue Gray contests,
East-West and North-South Games, and the American Bowl
from Tampa, Florida. In December 1974, he provided the
Mutual network radio coverage from the Sugar Bowl in New
Orleans, "which seemed like two games between the oppo-
nents." After trailing 10–0 for the first three periods,
Nebraska scored 13 fourth-quarter points and edged the
underdog Florida, 13–10.

During the summer of 1953 Jack televised his fourth consecutive All-Star Baseball Game. New assignments included
the Wednesday night stock car races from Santa Fe Park and
the beginning of a twenty-four-year radio commitment with
the Chicago Bears.

Throughout his Chicago career Jack made many return
visits to his Peoria hometown. He was—and still is—a wel-
comed celebrity, throwing the first ball at old-timers' baseball games and as a guest on radio and television programs.
One of the grandest events in which he participated was the
1954 ceremony at which *Look* magazine proclaimed Peoria
one of its "All-American" cities. ABC news analyst Paul Har-

Young Jack

Daisy and Will Brickhouse,
1915

Jack in Clarksville, Tennessee, age six

Interviewing boxer Jack Dempsey with Peoria sports promoter
Clyde Garrison, 1937

Hosting a WMBD entertainment program

Marine Corps Private Brickhouse in San Diego,
California, 1943

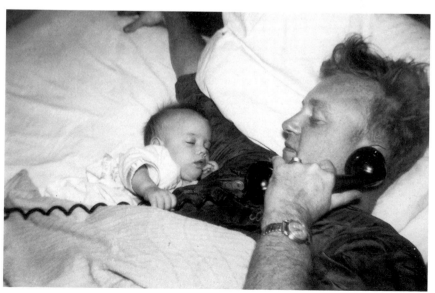

A working rest with daughter, Jeanne

Playtime with daughter, Jeanne

Brickhouse's was the first voice heard on WGN-TV, when in March 1948 he broadcast the Golden Gloves tournament from Chicago Stadium.

Chicago broadcasters at a 1948 charity softball game: in the dark shirt, Ernie Simon; dark sweater, Ed McElroy; light jacket, Bob Elson, with his arm on usher-service owner Andy Frain; plaid shirt, Linn Burton; front row, in front of Frain, Vince Garrity. Brickhouse is third from right in the Cubs cap, and Bob Finnegan is in front of Brickhouse. (Photo by Clyde W. White)

At the 1951 All-Star Game with Hall of Fame outfielder Tris Speaker
(Photo by George Brace)

At the 1959 World Series at Los Angeles Coliseum: interviewing White Sox
players Luis Aparicio and Al Smith (above) and with Giants owner Horace
Stoneham and Dodgers owner Walter O'Malley

Brickhouse shows his pitching form to Carl Erskine and Harvey Kuenn.

At Comiskey Park with Mickey Mantle

With Alvin Dark and fellow broadcaster Vince Lloyd

At Comiskey Park with
Babe Ruth, 1947

With White Sox manager Paul Richards during a pregame show called
"Baseball with the Girls," in the early 1950s (Photo courtesy of WGN-TV)

In the Comiskey Park
booth in the 1960s
(Photo by Tony Romano,
courtesy of WGN-TV)

Covering a game in the 1960s (Photo courtesy of WGN-TV)

Eddie Hubbard and Brickhouse interviewing Hollywood actress Joan
Crawford on the "Brickhouse-Hubbard Show," 1965

Celebrating the one thousandth "Bozo's Circus" on WGN-TV: from left,
Sandy the Clown, Don Sandburg; Bozo, Bob Bell; Ringmaster, Ned Locke;
Brickhouse; Oliver O. Oliver, Ray Rayner

Variety Club co–"Kings of Hearts" Brickhouse
and Irv Kupcinet

Jack Brickhouse, newspaper columnist (*Chicago's American* photo)

Lou Boudreau golfing with a bat and ball at North Shore Country Club, observed by fellow broadcasters Brickhouse and Jack Quinlan and Cubs general manager Bob Kennedy (*Chicago's American* photo)

Making a Hamm's beer commercial with Harry Creighton (center) in Minnesota, "the land of sky-blue waters"

vey and Dr. George Gallup, president of the National Municipal League and founder of the Gallup poll, were among the speakers at the two-hour award presentation. As master of ceremonies Jack entertained the thousand guests, introduced the speakers, and read congratulatory telegrams from old friends and former Peorians Charles Correll of "Amos 'n' Andy," Marian and Jim Jordan of "Fibber McGee and Molly," and Jack Sterling of CBS-TV in New York.

In the fall of 1954 Brickhouse was again on the NBC-TV team for the World Series, between the New York Giants and the Cleveland Indians. Telecast to about 150 American stations and eight Canadian outlets, the contest was made memorable by Giants centerfielder Willie Mays, who that season led the league with a .345 batting average and 41 home runs.

In the first game of the Series, with the score tied, the Indians' Vic Wertz hit a drive to deep center field that to baseball historian Robert Smith "would have been a long home run in any park in the world except the Polo Grounds, where the centerfield fence was something just short of half a mile from home plate." Mays, with his back to the infield, made a spectacular catch that saved two runs and brought the Indians' rally to a dead stop. At the microphone Jack broadcast what became known in baseball lore as "the catch." Forty years later writer J. Ronald Oakley described it as "an unbelievable play, often regarded as the best outfield catch in the history of baseball."

The Series became a "walkaway," with Cleveland losing in four games—the first National League sweep since 1914. Afterward Yankee manager Stengel dismissed the Giants as "not a great team . . . we would have murdered them."

Variety commended the work of Brickhouse and Hodges, who "neatly blended the word picture into the overall video scene. Their verbal offerings were pleasant, properly pitched and kept watchers abreast of the happenings with a full account of highlights of the action on the field, in the dugouts and, when the occasion presented itself, in the stands."

The next World Series assignment for Jack would come several years later and would involve a Chicago team.

CHAPTER 5

The White Sox—
and 1959

BEGINNING IN 1940, BRICKHOUSE BROADCAST THE BASE-ball games of both major-league Chicago teams for nearly thirty years. The White Sox assignment included television coverage of a rarity, a Windy City team in the World Series.

In his first year Jack was assistant to WGN broadcaster Bob Elson, "which meant doing the seventh inning while he took a rest or, if it was a doubleheader, doing the late innings so he could get out early."

> I'll never forget my first game, a doubleheader at Sox Park on a Sunday afternoon. Elson said, "You take the last couple of innings, I want to leave." I think I had worked three outs when all of a sudden everybody started walking off the field. I didn't know what was going on. The sun was still shining, but the plate umpire called the game.
>
> I was terrified. I was faking it anyway, because I'm up from Peoria and hadn't seen that many games,

especially major-league games. And there I was, all
by myself except for the engineer, and in those days
he didn't know any baseball at all.

I said to myself, "What else could it be but darkness?" Then I'm saying it on the air, and as it turned
out, I guessed right. The next day the papers really
took on the umpire for his call.

That summer longtime Sox owner J. Louis Comiskey
died, leaving the club in trust for his teenage son, Charles A.
II. The elder Comiskey's widow, Grace, became president and
operated the team with the assistance of her daughters and
son-in-law John D. Rigney, who had been a Sox pitcher.
Then, within months of the Japanese attack on Pearl Harbor, several of manager Jimmy Dykes's players left for military service. In midseason 1942, when Elson enlisted in the
navy, Brickhouse inherited sole possession of the broadcast
booth for the rest of the year and all of 1943.

Visiting with the players, Jack learned that shortstop
Luke Appling—who went on to win the 1943 American
League batting title—was asked by the Red Cross in his
Atlanta, Georgia, hometown for autographed baseballs to sell
at a wartime fund-raiser. "So, Luke asked the Sox for a couple dozen baseballs. While he was getting ready for batting
practice, he got the word that club vice president Harry Grabiner had turned him down—'Can't spare them.' Luke sent
the messenger back to tell Grabiner, 'You'd better come out
and watch my batting practice.' Grabiner went and watched
as Luke fouled twelve straight pitches into the seats. On the
last one Grabiner yelled, 'You've got them. You can have the
baseballs!'"

After the season Jack joined the Marine Corps but in 1945 had a new opportunity with the Sox, freelance broadcasting on WJJD and WIND. "The FCC had made a ruling against owning two stations in the same major market, so Ralph Atlass, owner of both stations, kept WIND, which had a better dial position and carried the Cubs. He sold WJJD to Marshall Field, who got the White Sox with it and who then asked me to do their games. But WJJD was a daytime-only station—it went off the air at sundown—so the Sox night games were carried on WIND, which was permitted."

The 1945 White Sox were far from impressive with only 22 home runs in the entire season, while the city's other team was on its way to the National League championship. "I'm working at WJJD in the Carbide and Carbon Building on Michigan Avenue. It's August; we're doing the road games by ticker, with, of course, no air-conditioning in the studio. I'm trying to hold the audience with the White Sox playing Connie Mack's Philadelphia Athletics, battling for seventh place. Through the open window you could hear the Cubs up the street winning a pennant!"

Toward the end of the season Elson returned from the service and reclaimed his position with the Sox. Jack broadcast New York Giants baseball for one year and back in Chicago did the 1947 Cubs games on WBKB-TV. "And then, along came WGN television. General manager Frank Schreiber wanted me for their baseball and other sports—and I've been there ever since."

The first major-league telecast on WGN-TV, Channel 9, was an April 1948 preseason White Sox–Cubs game. As WGN's sole baseball announcer on television that year, Jack broadcast both teams' entire home-game schedules to an estimated two million viewers. "I'd do a ball game in the afternoon, stop by the studio for the 6:00 sports, then go out five nights a week to broadcast wrestling or boxing. We were working seven-day weeks, but we sensed that we were on the ground floor of something tremendously important." Both Chicago baseball teams finished last in their leagues that year, the Sox losing 101 games.

Prior to the 1949 season young Charles Comiskey II took over the team, hiring as his general manager a sportswriter and Big Ten official, Frank Lane. Early in his tenure Lane made a series of successful trades, acquiring pitcher Billy Pierce and second baseman Nellie Fox, then outfielder Orestes "Minnie" Minoso and shortstop Luis Aparicio. With his new talent Lane managed the Sox in a steady ascent from nearly two decades of losing seasons.

Jack described his friendship with Lane to team historian Bob Vanderberg: "In fact," said Jack, "I got Frank an apartment in my building, near Surf and Sheridan Road. Frank and I would drive home together many times." Jack also discussed "Home Run Lane"—a $5,000 wire fence that Lane installed in left field during his first season "to increase home-run production [and] create a little more fun at the old ballpark." But after opposing players hit 11 home runs in eight games, Jack told Vanderberg, he "kind of figured" the days of Lane's fence were numbered:

> I'm driving Lane home and he's boiling. He is just absolutely frying. We're driving up Lake Shore Drive past Oak Street Beach. I said, "Frank, don't worry about it. Take your mind off it. Take a look at all those beautiful girls out there in their bathing suits. I'll do the driving, and you can do the looking." But in order to see them, he had to look

through another wire fence. He finally yelled, "All I can see is that lousy fence! Can't even enjoy this!"

And so now we get home, and about one o'clock in the morning, after he'd been stewing and fretting about it all night long, I guess you know he got poor Leo Dillon, the maintenance chief, out of bed and whipped that crew out there to that ballpark in the middle of the night, and that fence was DOWN by the time the Yankees came out to the ballpark the next day. And Phil Rizzuto, who never hit any home runs, told me, "Even I was licking my chops—we came out and saw that fence was gone, we were really burned up."

The 1949 and 1950 Sox teams avoided the cellar of 1948, yet the improvements were marginal. In 1951 Lane named minor-league manager Paul Richards as his field manager. To Jack, "Richards had a really fine baseball mind. You'd sit there and almost see the wheels go around. He had that look of the eagle—that wiry, leathery, muscular look. No one could reclaim pitchers better than Richards."

Jack was impressed with rookie Venezuelan shortstop Alfonso "Chico" Carrasquel, Lane's choice to replace "Old Aches and Pains" Appling. "Chico was one of Lane's best purchases; he managed to claim him from the Dodgers for $25,000. And Chico had a fantastic season. I don't recall many players having as good a first year; then he slowed down. In recent years he's been the team's Spanish-language broadcaster."

The 1951–59 White Sox were characterized by writer Richard Lindberg as a "sequence of winning teams," combining pitching with defense and speed to finish consistently in the first division. "They could bunt, steal bases, take extra bases, and literally run circles around the opposition. Even when they weren't stealing bases, the opposing pitcher thought they were going to and couldn't concentrate."

In 1951 a strong performance by rookie Nellie Fox (only 11 strikeouts in more than 600 at-bats), along with league-leading triples and stolen bases from Minoso, led fans to a chant of "Go! Go! Sox!" Fox and Carrasquel were starters in the All-Star Game, but an extended losing streak soon after midseason dashed the pennant prospects. Both that year and the next the Sox finished with identical 81–73 records. Catcher Sherm Lollar and outfielder "Jungle Jim" Rivera joined the team in 1952 and would be integral to its success for a number of years.

Early in the 1953 season the *Tribune*'s Anton Remenih reported that Brickhouse had already "collided with his annual problem: Should he mention a no hitter in the making, or should he respect baseball hoodoo laws and keep silent? 'If I do [mention that a pitcher has allowed no hits] and later a player gets one, fans accuse me of jinxing the team. If I don't, others take me apart for keeping secret the most important fact about the ball game.' "

Remenih described a Sox game against the St. Louis Browns in which Jack "first mentioned the possibility of a perfect game at the end of the sixth inning." Then, with two out in the seventh, Pierce gave up a double to the Browns' second baseman. According to Remenih, Jack had conducted two polls on the question. "The first, four years ago, showed that eight out of nine fans voted against reporting a potential no hitter. He repeated the survey last season and this time the vote was reversed—eight out of nine wanted to know about it." Jack felt that television was primarily responsible for the change in attitude: "or what is probably more accurate, it has created a new batch [of fans], mostly women and children, who don't go along with old timers' taboos."

The 1953 Sox improved to 89–65, and for the second consecutive year Minoso led the league in stolen bases. That fall Jack was featured in the Sunday *Tribune*, described as "television's busiest sports announcer," earning more than $1,000 weekly, "and one of the happiest men alive."

Preparing for the 1954 season, the Sox acquired veteran Phil Cavarretta, a Brickhouse friend from Three-I baseball in Peoria and two decades with the Cubs. And on Jack's recommendation WGN-TV hired Peoria newspaper reporter Jack Rosenberg as a sportswriter and statistician. Brickhouse was quoted in the *Tribune*: "There are a lot of radio-TV sports announcers who have statisticians . . . but as far as I know, Rosenberg is the lone sports writer in baseball writing human interest items for TV." Brickhouse claims, "Anything clever I ever said was probably written by Rosey."

Rosenberg told the *Tribune*: "When I was writing about Bradley University sports activities for the *Peoria Journal* and *Pekin Daily Times*, I had to write complete stories. Now, as a TV sports writer, I have to condense stories and anecdotes about players in two or three terse sentences so Brickhouse can weave them into his play-by-play during a lull in the game."

Chuck Wenk, an assistant to Bob Elson at WJJD, later reminisced in the *Milwaukee Journal* about Brickhouse and his television staff of Rosenberg, Bob Foster, and Jack Jacobson:

> We were all doing the Sox games. . . . Brickhouse played every trick in the book on Elson and our radio booth. Even though Bob was instrumental in bringing Jack up from Peoria and to WGN, not

a day went by that the TV crew of Rosenberg-Fos-
ter-Jacobson didn't try and trap us into some goofy
mistake.

Never trusting our own crude wire system
from WJJD or WCFL, we always "snuck" items
from the WGN ticker or bootlegged "scoops" that
leaked through the plywood booth dividers.

Brickhouse would press his shut-off switch
and fake items like new baseball commissioners
(ranging from Joe E. Brown to Harry Grabiner),
new managers, celebrities in the stands, and
"scores" that were not available to us. . . . we were
consistently suckered and always following up
with a "correction."

The 1954 still-improving Sox were 94–60, their best season since 1920. Cavarretta batted .316 in a utility role but
was released early in 1955. That year Pierce led both leagues
with a 1.97 ERA and finished with a 15–10 record. Lane complained it was "the year the Sox should have won the pennant but didn't," then resigned in frustration after the team
led the league in hitting but finished in third place.

Over the winter Carrasquel was traded for power-hitting
outfielder Larry Doby, who in 1947 had been the first
African-American player in the American League (and in
1978 became the White Sox manager). On opening day of
the 1956 season Sox fan Richard J. Daley enjoyed his first
game as the mayor of Chicago. Aparicio, called up from
the minors to replace Carrasquel, impressed Brickhouse.
"Considering his bat, his glove, his competitive spirit, the way
he could take charge in a quiet way out there, the way he
could handle the double-play ball, the way he and Fox fit each
other like a glove on the double play—it was poetry in
motion."

During mid-June, in what was later termed the "biggest weekend of the fifties," the White Sox swept a four-game series from the 1955-champion Yankees. Pierce, with a 9–2 midseason record, was named starting pitcher in the All-Star Game, then became the first Sox 20-game winner in fifteen years. Aparicio led the American League in stolen bases and was voted Rookie of the Year.

Yet the season was another disappointment, for the Sox finished third behind New York and Cleveland. Marty Marion was replaced by former Cleveland manager Al Lopez, who in six years had led the Indians to one pennant and five second-place finishes.

Early in the 1957 season the Sox held on to first place for several weeks. On June 13 from Comiskey Park, Jack reported on "the greatest baseball fight I ever saw. Seldom in such incidents does anyone really get hurt, but this was a rough one." Yankee pitcher Art Ditmar had aimed a fastball at Doby, then mumbled a racial slur; Doby rushed to the mound and decked Ditmar with "a quick left." Both benches were emptied, and New York outfielder Enos Slaughter later described the ensuing thirty-minute brawl as "the best he had seen in twenty years in baseball."

Slaughter took on Sox first baseman Walt Dropo, and, according to Jack: "When it was over, Slaughter started back to the bench, his shirt in shreds. A *Tribune* photographer took an award-winning picture that he titled 'The Embattled Warrior.' On television I remarked, 'There's Enos Slaughter, whose opponent today was Walt Dropo, the biggest, strongest man in sports. But we shouldn't be surprised at Enos's courage—after all, he's been married five times!' "

Two weeks later *The Sporting News* placed the fight in historical perspective:

Ninety-four and one-half years after Abe Lincoln
delivered his Emancipation Proclamation, baseball
the other day witnessed the complete emancipation of the American Negro in America's national
game.

Larry Doby, a colored player of the White
Sox, dared to take a punch at Art Ditmar, a white
pitcher of the Yankees, and history was being
made. Never before in the 11 years since the bars
were dropped and colored players admitted, albeit
gingerly, to the major leagues, had a Negro thrown
the first punch in a player argument.

There is no intent here to condone what Doby
did; merely to point out that the consequences fell
far short of Civil War, or secession, or a violent
sense of outrage except among Ditmar's Yankee
teammates who dashed to his assistance, but in no
more anger than if his attacker had been a white
player. . . .

Now this was no white pitcher dusting off a
Negro batter simply because of the difference in
pigmentation. . . . But the Doby-Ditmar episode
had special significance because for the first time
a Negro player was daring to get as assertive as
the white man whose special province Organized
Ball had been for nearly a hundred years.

After their strong early-season performance, the Sox
folded in the stretch but still ended in second place. Mayor
Daley confidently predicted a championship team for Chicago
in 1958, even though both Doby and Minoso had left the Sox
in off-season trades. To Brickhouse, "Daley was a great
Chicago sports fan and Sox fan. Every time we met at a public function, he would pump me dry with questions about
the teams."

In June of 1958 Brickhouse broadcast a Sox game against the Washington Senators in which Pierce pitched a perfect game until the last out in the ninth inning. Relief catcher Ed Fitz Gerald, pinch hitting for the pitcher, "sliced a double into right field, just out of Ray Boone's reach at first base. Then the next batter struck out." And according to Jerome Holtzman in the *Sun-Times*, after the game Pierce "kept repeating, 'I won! I'm thankful for that.'"

Late in the season *Chicago's American* reported that Brickhouse, covering both the Sox and the Cubs, "chalked up a new record—his 1,500th telecast of a regular season major league game," a figure achieved by "no other sportscaster in the country." The Sox, however, again finished in second place.

In March 1959, after a series of court struggles, the Comiskey family—White Sox owners since the team joined the American League in 1901—sold their controlling interest to a syndicate that included promoter William Veeck, Jr. To Chicago author Kenan Heise, Veeck was "what P. T. Barnum wished to be—the consummate hustler. . . . The little things, from not wearing a tie to sitting in the bleachers, made Bill Veeck a shining example of a man of the people."

In his first Sox season Veeck had billboards placed around the city proclaiming, "We will bring a pennant to Chicago." He nurtured the Go! Go! team, combining tenacious defense with swift baserunning. Hitting came later in the year, when first baseman Ted Kluszewski joined the club.

And manager Al Lopez on the bench was wringing every drop of talent from his boys. He had endless patience, the greatest example of which may have been with one of his catcher-outfielders. In need of a

third baseman, Lopez worked tirelessly with Bubba
Phillips.

That spring, and the spring before it, down in
Tampa where the White Sox trained, Lopez himself
must have hit a thousand ground balls to Phillips.
Lopez would just stand there by the hour and hit
grounders to Bubba, moving him to his left, to his
right, then back, and then making him come in—just
wore him out. Lopez hit so many doggone ground
balls to Bubba that fielding anything became second
nature to him.

Veeck amused his Comiskey Park fans—sending clowns
to the coaching lines, hosting cow-milking contests, dusting
off home plate with a vacuum cleaner. At a game honoring
outfielder Al Smith, Veeck granted free admission to fans
named Smith. To Jack the team's owner was "a believer in
the 'fun at the old ballpark' theme. He had all sorts of ideas.
I loved the time a helicopter landed a group of midgets
dressed as Martians, who captured Aparicio and Fox and
carted them off the playing field. Veeck enjoyed the circus
atmosphere if he could create it, but he knew as well as anybody that there's no substitute for winning."

In late July the Sox ended a forty-year drought—claim-
ing first place in the league and holding on for the rest of the
season. In his autobiography Veeck described what happened
in 1959:

> We had a team that had no right at all to win the
> pennant. We were a club that knew every time we
> went out on the field that we couldn't possibly win
> by more than two runs. By all logic, we were the

ones who should have been playing scared. What
happened was exactly the reverse. . . . We'd win
one day on a swinging bunt, the next day on a
passed ball, and the day after that when somebody would lose a fly in the sun. . . .

Everybody kept saying how lucky we were
and, up to a point, we were. The point where luck
ceased to be the prime factor was the point where
our own confidence—which was far greater than
our skill—took over.

"Those Sox were a fun bunch to watch," Jack recalls.
"They'd beat you, 2–1. A big rally for them consisted of an
infield single, a stolen base, a passed ball, and a sacrifice fly.
They had great pitching, a hell of a manager, and marvelous
defense—just a very enchanting team."

The Sox clinched the pennant on September 22 in Cleveland. The *Tribune* reported that on the charter flight to
Chicago Jack "paced the aisles lining up interviews" for a
live broadcast. Arriving at Chicago's Midway Airport at
2:00 A.M., the team was greeted by a crowd estimated by
some at thirty thousand—by Veeck at three hundred thousand. Mayor Daley, who had watched the deciding game on
television, "was up the landing ramp steps the instant the first
of the White Sox appeared." In celebration he and Fire Commissioner Bob Quinn decided to turn on the city's one hundred air-raid sirens. Many residents—"mostly Cub fans"
according to Jack—panicked and scrambled for cover, fear-
ing a Soviet invasion.

In achieving their first pennant since 1919, the year of the
Black Sox scandal, the Sox won 35 games by only one run.
Pitcher Early Wynn, acquired in the Minoso trade, won the
Cy Young Award with a 22–10 record. Aparicio stole 56

bases, the most in the major leagues since 1943. Fox was named Most Valuable Player, with Aparicio and Wynn in second and third place.

The National League championship was claimed by the Dodgers, in their second year on the West Coast. Even though the Dodgers led their league in fielding, strikeouts, bullpen saves, and stolen bases, the Sox were favored to win the World Series.

The NBC television network and its sponsor, the Gillette Safety Razor Company, selected the Series announcers. Lindsey Nelson, NBC assistant director of sports, explained to author Curt Smith, "Believe me, we took great pride—painstaking care—in our choice of announcers. Back then, the Series was the blue-chip event in all of sports. Nothing rivaled it. Nothing was remotely *close*."

As the Dodgers' lead announcer, Vin Scully was an anticipated choice by both NBC and Gillette. But according to Nelson, the selection of Brickhouse was more involved, the result of NBC sports director Thomas Gallery's "absolute disdain" for Bob Elson, the White Sox radio broadcaster. Nelson recalled Gallery's dilemma: "I said to him, 'Well, Tom, you may have an out. Jack Brickhouse is the principal TV guy for both the Cubs and White Sox. You could always pick him.' And Gallery's face lit up like a Christmas tree. He thought Brickhouse was a class act—which, of course, he is. So that's what Tom did, chose Brickhouse to go along with Scully." With that, Jack received his fourth World Series broadcast assignment.

At Comiskey Park the first game fulfilled Sox fans' dreams, as Wynn and the thirty-five-year-old slugger Ted Kluszewski spearheaded an 11–0 victory. Afterward Veeck told a reporter, "In the third inning, when we scored seven

runs, I almost left. I thought I'd gotten into the wrong park."
The jubilation was short-lived, however, for in the second
game, with Democratic presidential nominee John F. Kennedy
among the fans, the Dodgers evened the series in a close 4–3
contest.

Each of the next three games in Los Angeles drew record
crowds of more than ninety-two thousand to Memorial Coliseum, converted temporarily from a football and track-and-
field stadium. In games three and four, Larry Sherry provided
strong relief pitching for the Dodgers—while the Sox squan-
dered numerous scoring opportunities, losing 3–1 and 5–4.

To Jack "the fifth game, at the Coliseum—that's my
biggest memory, the most exciting game of the Series. With
the Dodgers holding a 3–1 edge, the Sox have to win to bring
it back to Chicago." In the fourth inning the Sox took a 1–0
lead on Dodger pitcher Sandy Koufax with singles by Fox
and Jim Landis and a double-play ball by Lollar. In the seventh the Dodgers threatened—with two on, two out, and
Charlie Neal at bat. Jack described the situation: "Lopez
called time. He switched his left- and rightfielders, putting
Jim Rivera, the better and faster defensive player, in right.
Sure enough, Neal hit into the right-center-field gap. Left-
handed Rivera, with a great jump on the ball, made a dead
on-the-run catch to end the inning. And, by golly, the Sox
made that one-run margin stand up—to me, a win that has
never been topped for tenseness, emotion, and excitement."

Sox starter Bob Shaw and relievers Pierce and Dick
Donovan combined in the game for the first three-pitcher
shutout in Series history.

Back in Chicago, the cheers of nearly forty-eight thousand fans changed to frustration as Dodgers batters routed
Wynn. With an 8–3 lead in the ninth inning, Chuck Essegian

pinch hit for home-run hitter Duke Snider and smashed his own homer—his second of the Series and a pinch-hitting record. The Dodgers took the contest in six games.

"A good Series" in the estimation of Brickhouse and the closest the Sox would come to a world championship with their veteran broadcaster. He and Scully were honored by *Look* magazine for their broadcast coverage. The *Chicago Tribune*'s Herb Lyon wrote: "Everywhere I go I hear comment about Commentator Jack Brickhouse's remarkable restraint in reporting the series on TV so ultra-objectively. Quite a trick for a rabid, unreconstructed Sox fan."

The White Sox remained a competitive first-division team in the American League through 1967. With the exception of the New York Yankees, no other American League club could make the claim, nor would any other contemporary Chicago sports team come close to the Sox's winning record.

The team held spring training in Sarasota, Florida, and each year Jack broadcast some of the games.

> In March of one year I went to telecast a Sunday afternoon Sox-Yankee exhibition game. It was what we call a *split feed*. Mel Allen and Phil Rizzuto were the Yankee broadcasters doing the feed for their New York station, and I was doing it for WGN.
>
> The tower at the top of a hotel in Bradenton, Florida, up the road a piece, was blown down, so we lost the television picture—all we had was audio. Allen and Rizzuto decided they were not going on the air until the picture was back. I took the position that we had spent a lot of money and gone to a lot of trou-

ble to get this pickup, so we would do the audio—
an old-fashioned radio thing—and describe the action
until the picture came back.

It didn't come back for *an hour*. For nearly the
first five innings we were without a picture. But about
our ratings: One service gave us a fifteen—we wiped
out the closest competitor in Chicago, WBBM, with a
seven. Another rating service was a little more real-
istic, coming up with a two or three. It was either a
marvelous tribute to baseball or a real raised eyebrow
that with no picture for an hour we got a fifteen
rating.

For the 1960 season only Fox and Pierce remained from
the 1951 beginning of the Go! Go! era. On opening day
Minoso, who was reacquired during the off-season, celebrated with a grand slam and then a solo home run, chris-
tening Comiskey Park's new $300,000 exploding musical
scoreboard—another of Veeck's innovations. After a strong
start, however, the team fell to third place, while breaking
the attendance record set in the previous year's championship
drive.

The American League expanded in 1961, adding the California Angels and Washington Senators (the previous Senators having become the Minnesota Twins). The Sox opened
the season against the new Senators at Griffith Stadium,
with President Kennedy guesting on Vince Lloyd's pregame
show and then throwing the first ball. Even though Aparicio led the league in stolen bases, the rest of the team lacked
speed, and by July they were in last place. Richard Lindberg
wrote that the Go! Go! Sox had become the Slow-Slow Sox.
An ailing Veeck sold the team to Chicago businessmen

Arthur C. Allyn, Jr., and his brother John Allyn. Then a 12-game winning streak brought the Sox back into the first division; they finished fourth in the ten-team league—their worst finish since 1951.

Prior to the 1962 season the Sox traded both Minoso and Pierce. The last Comiskey-owned shares of stock were purchased by a group of young Chicagoans, who the following year sold out to the Allyns. For the first time in the lengthy White Sox history, the Comiskey family was not associated with ownership or management of the team.

By the end of the 1963 season, forty-two-year-old Wynn had accumulated 299 career victories. Released from the team in November, he achieved the "magic 300" with Cleveland the next summer. Also in 1963, Nellie Fox, the last of the Go! Go! Sox, made his 2,500th career hit but after the season was sold to Houston.

On August 7, 1964, the twenty-fifth wedding anniversary of Jack and Nelda Brickhouse, he telecast a Sox-Orioles game during the day and the All-Star Football Game that evening. Later in the month he covered both the Democratic and Republican national political conventions. Then, in early September, nearly a month after the anniversary, their fifteen-year-old daughter, Jeanne, hosted a huge surprise celebration at a Chicago restaurant.

In the final days of the season the Yankees streaked to their fifth straight league title. The Sox won their last nine games, finishing one game behind New York and leading the majors with a 2.72 ERA. Former Sox pitcher Billy Pierce retired in 1964 after three years with the San Francisco Giants, and Jack remarked: "In my many years covering baseball, I've reported thousands of strikeouts, but the one I regret most is the one that never happened. My friend Billy Pierce finished his career with 1,999 strikeouts. I would have given a lot to have seen him wind up with number two thousand."

In 1965 the Sox season began splendidly—22 wins in the first 30 games. Rookie Tommy John won 14 games during the season, but the team again ended in second place. Lopez resigned as manager to accept a vice presidential post with the Sox. In seventeen years as a major-league manager his teams all finished in the first division. Former St. Louis manager Eddie Stanky was hired to replace Lopez on the field.

During the 1966 season centerfielder Tommie Agee hit 22 home runs and stole 44 bases to win Rookie of the Year, yet the team fell to a fourth-place finish with the worst team batting average in the majors. Not surprisingly, season attendance fell below one million—for only the second time in seventeen years.

In 1967 Jack broadcast a White Sox no-hitter, the first game of a doubleheader with Detroit. "What I remember most about that gem by Joel Horlen was that the Tigers' Jerry Lumpe almost beat out an infield roller in the ninth, an eyelash play at first. But then the ninth inning of any no-hitter is pulsating."

In the middle of the 1967 season, with the team in first place, Sox owner Arthur Allyn announced a multiyear contract with Field Enterprises and WFLD, Chicago's first UHF television station. Jack recalls that "WFLD made a big offer to the White Sox, and as a result, at the end of the 1967 season the Sox said good-bye to WGN and to Jack Brickhouse":

On paper the offer looked great, a five-year deal with a five-year option, for a lot more money than WGN-TV had offered. Allyn thought, I'll have my own station; I won't have to share time with the Cubs.

But it turned out to be a *bad* idea. WFLD was a

UHF station; anything above Channel 12 was UHF. It was not as reliable as VHF, especially in the summertime, because its low-carrying sound waves could not penetrate the foliage on trees and bushes. Also, in those days, a lot of sets couldn't get UHF without a special adaptor. One of the reasons WFLD wanted the White Sox was that viewers who wanted to see the games had to buy the adaptors.

But the White Sox did not play good ball those years, and the Cubs were somewhat better. We killed them in the ratings. They were getting asterisks, we were getting fifteens, twenties, twenty-twos. Today, my gosh, that's unbelievable. After the first five years WFLD was taking such a beating that they didn't take the second five-year option.

Then, in 1969, Arthur Allyn sold his portion of the Sox to his brother John. According to Jack:

We had been friends, golfing buddies, for one thing, before Arthur and John ever got in the baseball business. But John simply could not do any good with the team. I helped him get on some small radio stations around the area, but he still wound up in financial trouble. In 1975 he felt that he had to sell the ball club. He did not want it moved from Chicago; he felt that obligation. I saw his offer letter from a Seattle promoter, Lester Smith, who had a group of investors, one of whom was the entertainer Danny Kaye. They offered $10 million for the team.

I was determined not to let the White Sox leave this town. I worked on putting together a group to buy it from John at that $10 million price. I had a good job at Channel 9; I suppose I would have had to quit if I had taken on the Sox. Instead Bill Veeck got back into the act. He decided that he wanted to buy the team, and he organized a group of investors. When I asked, "How are you doing?" he said, "I'm short." Even though several other team owners put severe restrictions and requirements on his purchase, Veeck kept plugging away. The night before the deadline I was able to deliver the funds from my group to Veeck. And he never turned down a chance to thank me publicly for that.

According to Veeck biographer Gerald Eskenazi:

> It had become a civic affair. Jack Brickhouse, the Chicago television personality, actually helped get Veeck together with his new investor. He was Patrick L. O'Malley, and his reasons for becoming involved spotlighted what a team can mean to a city. "We wanted to do our part to save this franchise for Chicago," explained O'Malley. "I've seen what happened to other communities losing sports teams. I remember back when New York lost the Dodgers and Giants, and the city really lost some of its sports heritage."

Brickhouse is modestly pleased that his involvement kept the Sox in Chicago, adding, "In 1991 I was flattered to help dedicate the new Comiskey Park and the Bill Veeck press box."

CHAPTER 6

The Cubs—
and 1969

D URING THE 1945 WORLD SERIES BETWEEN THE Chicago Cubs and the Detroit Tigers, an unfortunate Wrigley Field incident may have caused the Cubs irreparable bad luck. William Sianis, owner of the Billy Goat Tavern and an avid Cubs fan, bought game tickets for himself and his prize-winning goat Sonovia, only to be turned away by the stadium ushers. His cheer turning quickly to rage, Sianis retaliated by placing an eternal hex on the Cubs—who went on to lose the Series in seven games. It was the last time the team has played in a World Series. And Jack Brickhouse, broadcaster for the Cubs from 1940 through 1943 and again from 1947 through 1981, was given the honor by the *Chicago Tribune*'s Steve Daley of having "seen more bad baseball than any person, living or dead."

For five decades the Brickhouse name was synonymous with the Chicago Cubs—from his first assignment as broadcasting assistant on WGN radio, to the first Wrigley Field telecast in 1947, through his last official game in 1981 and many subsequent appearances for the team.

His first year with the Cubs, 1940, was the final one for
their All-Star pitcher Dizzy Dean—a season that saw the
team finish in the second division for the first time in fifteen
years. The following season brought the Cubs a colorful
rookie, Louis Novikoff, known as the "Mad Russian." In the
minor league Novikoff had been called "another Babe Ruth,
hitting anything he could reach with his bat." As a Cub, he
"became the subject of more words on sports pages than all
the other baseball players combined." To Jack, Novikoff was
a "bona fide character":

> Novikoff had been an almost world-famous softball
> player and came to the Cubs from their minor-league
> team in Los Angeles. In those days the Cubs had a
> midnight curfew because the games were usually
> played in the afternoons. If a player violated the cur-
> few, it cost him one day's pay.
>
> This was during the Big Band era, and there was
> a famous nightclub right outside of Philadelphia on
> the Thompson Turnpike. The Cubs' traveling secre-
> tary was Bobby Lewis, one of the funniest men I've
> ever known—he should have been in vaudeville. One
> time on a Philadelphia and Pittsburgh swing, Lewis
> and the Cubs' manager Jimmie Wilson were in their
> hotel room, which didn't have any air-conditioning.
> They had the fan on, sitting in their shorts—trying
> to stay cool, listening to the radio.
>
> On came the announcer with the Big Band broad-
> cast: "Now, ladies and gentlemen, as part of our fea-
> ture from the Thompson Turnpike, we happen to
> have the very famous outfielder for the Chicago Cubs,
> Lou Novikoff, who will now favor us by singing his
> rendition of 'Trees.' " Wilson and Lewis looked at

their watches, and it was already midnight. Lewis said, "Don't you think we should catch the one o'clock show?"

They put on their clothes and took a cab to the nightclub. According to Lewis, when they walked in the place, Novikoff was on about his tenth encore of "Trees." Well, it cost him a day's pay. And just the night before he had been nailed in Pittsburgh for violating curfew.

Later Lewis asked him, "Why don't you do it smarter, Lou? What does your wife say when the checks come in every first and fifteenth docked like this?" All Novikoff could think to say was, "Bobby, how was I to know you were going to check up on me two nights in a row?"

Years earlier, around 1930, Lewis had had a running feud with Hack Wilson, the famous Cubs outfielder and one of the great hitters of all time (he still holds the record for runs batted in, 190, and the National League record for home runs, 56). Hack had a genuine contempt for the curfew. He and some of the other ballplayers lived in an apartment hotel up on North Sheridan Road, not far from Wrigley Field. They had to be at the ballpark by something like 11:00 in the morning. Otherwise they were in trouble, and again we're talking about a day's pay.

Wilson got to the ballpark real late one day, and he was fined. When he went back to the hotel, he raised Cain with the switchboard operator: "You know I have a permanent call here at 9:00 in the morning! Why didn't you wake me up instead of letting me get nailed like this?" Her answer, "But Mr. Wilson, you didn't get in until 10:00."

The Cubs and Novikoff finished his rookie season again in the second division. That fall owner Philip K. Wrigley made plans for installing lights in the ballpark. According to his biographer Paul Angle:

> The year was 1941, and the defense industry was humming night and day. In President Roosevelt's opinion, factory workers needed relaxation. Among other things, he suggested an increase in night baseball so that workers on day shifts would have an opportunity to see more games. Wrigley responded by ordering the necessary equipment. By December 1, it was all assembled and ready for installation. On Sunday, December 7, Japanese bombers attacked Pearl Harbor. The next day the Cub management offered everything—towers, lights, cables—to the U.S. government, which immediately accepted the offer.

Nearly half a century later, in a 1988 ABC-TV program on the new night lighting at Wrigley Field, Jack spoke to reporter Judd Rose about the 1941 situation. "Along came a little thing called Pearl Harbor, and that took care of that. After all, [Wrigley] was not about to let something as critical as that type of material be used for something that's as comparatively unimportant as baseball."

Wrigley's biographer continued: "And so the Cubs . . . faced the war years. . . . They would be years of ragged baseball, but they would also be years of innovations, abysmal failure, and triumph." Among the innovations was the installation of the first major-league ballpark organ. In 1942 the team won just 68 games—its poorest showing since 1925—and the 1943 season was little better.

When Jack returned from military service in 1944 and found that WGN was not broadcasting baseball that year, he concentrated on college sports and variety and public affairs programs. After the Cubs opened the season with 9 straight losses, manager Jimmie Wilson resigned. "I cannot explain the slump, but it is here," he said. "And in baseball, when you don't win, you have to get out." Wilson's replacement was the good-humored Charlie "Jolly Cholly" Grimm, who in the 1930s had both played for and managed the Cubs. Announcing Grimm's return, Wrigley said, "I never had anybody else in mind for the job . . . he was the best manager this club has ever had."

From 1941 through 1944 Novikoff was shuffled between Chicago and the minor league, his performance both at the plate and in the field disappointing. As reported in the Wrigley biography, Grimm considered Novikoff "a terrific showman. . . . But unfortunately he was just one of those guys that could never do a job in the major leagues. He was a very erratic fielder—defensively he was a bad ball player, but he put on a show for you. The fans loved it."

For the 1945 baseball season Jack worked exclusively for the White Sox—the year the Cubs triumphed in the league but lost the World Series to Detroit. That autumn the Yankees announced the installation of lights for the 1946 season—leaving only Boston, Detroit, and Wrigley Field without night baseball: "We believe that baseball is a daytime sport," Wrigley told the *Tribune*, "and will continue to play it in the sunshine as long as we can." From 1921 to 1971 the Chicago Bears football team also played at Wrigley Field. "Right up through the 1960s," wrote E. M. Swift in *Sports Illustrated*, "there was talk of installing lights in Wrigley Field so the Chicago Bears could start their football games later in the day and the Cubs could finish games that otherwise would be called on account of darkness. But the Bears moved to Soldier Field, and Wrigley Field remained unchanged."

On radio with the New York Giants in 1946, Jack returned to Chicago in 1947. He telecast on WBKB, Channel 4, both the Cubs and the Sox—both losing teams. Forty years later he reminisced to Curt Smith,

> In those early days there wasn't a lot usually to cheer about *on* the field. But people watched anyway; why, I don't know. Mostly, I guess, because people loved the Cubs. They loved baseball. And in those first years, mostly, I suppose, because of the simple *fact* of TV—the fact that it existed. To people in those days, that in itself was stunning. People would sit and stare for hours, just gawking at the set.
>
> There were maybe 10,000 sets in Chicago, and about 7,000 of them were in saloons. I learned that each of those tiny barroom TV sets was being watched by an average of 25–35 people. The viewers wanted lots of talk, because the boys at the end of the bar needed eyes as keen as Ted Williams' to see the screen. Then when more sets came into the homes, and the number of viewers per set decreased, we got a different message from the viewers. They said, "Shut up, and don't talk so much."

Fellow broadcaster Curt Gowdy wrote that nothing changed sports "the way television did," beginning in the late 1940s. "It would pump in immense sums of money, enriching owners and players alike. It would have its negative side, too. Television devastated baseball's minor leagues: Why would you want to see a game of Class B ball when you could see the Giants play the Dodgers?" Gowdy concluded, "I don't think anybody could have foreseen those things . . . but they knew things weren't going to be the way they'd been before the war."

Major-league attendance plummeted as well in television's early years—from an all-time high of 20 million in 1948 to 14.4 million five years later. "The greatest fear I have about baseball is that we'll become a studio game," a concerned National League president Warren Giles said at the time. "We'll be playing with only 500 people in the stands and everybody else watching on TV."

Becoming WGN's manager of sports services early in 1948, Jack worked to bring the Cubs back from their 1944 move to WIND, which paid Wrigley $65,000 a year for the broadcasts. "Ward Quaal with WGN loved the game. We had the Cubs on television, and he wanted them on radio as well." Jack advised Quaal to offer $1 million for a five-year radio commitment: "You may lose a little at first, but by the third year you'll make money from then until eternity." Wrigley accepted the offer, effective with the 1948 season.

Months earlier WGN station manager Frank Schreiber had negotiated with both the White Sox and the Cubs to televise their home games. Then he lured Brickhouse away from WBKB-TV to be the broadcaster. "I was alone in the booth that first year doing Cubs' games—pregame, nine innings, extra innings, postgame, it was all me." The Cubs ended the 1948 season in last place, their worst finish since 1925.

For 1949 Jack was teamed with Harry Creighton in the booth, "the first in a parade" of Brickhouse partners over the next three and a half decades—partners that included Marty Hogan, Lou Boudreau, Lloyd Pettit, Jim West, Jack Quinlan, Len Johnson, Milo Hamilton, and Vince Lloyd. On

Brickhouse's recommendations Quinlan and Lloyd would both follow him on the WMBD-to-WGN, Peoria-to-Chicago connection, as had *Peoria Journal* reporter Jack Rosenberg.

In the 1994 book *Name of the Game: The Business of Sports*, the authors claim that good announcers could help hold attention "even when the fan's team is hopelessly behind." They reason that the broadcasters would develop relationships with their listeners: "There isn't a fan in the world who, while speeding through stations, won't stop at the sound of his or her favorite announcer." Over the decades Jack and his partners remained popular with Cubs fans even though the team played losing ball season after season.

In June 1949, Jack's broadcasting successor with the New York Giants, Frank Frisch, succeeded the beleaguered Grimm as Cubs manager. A few days later outfielder Hank Sauer joined the team from Cincinnati: "Frisch told me, 'Hank, we brought you here for just one reason, to hit homers and drive in runs.' And I did exactly what he wanted," with five consecutive 30-homer seasons.

Among Jack's recollections from the early television days was his first—and slowest—triple play:

> One of the best actions in baseball is a triple play, and of course it generally happens very fast. I've been lucky to see a few—not many, because there aren't many. The first one I saw took about thirty seconds. The Cubs were playing the Pittsburgh Pirates at Wrigley Field. Frankie Gustine was the Pittsburgh third baseman, and Clyde McCullough was the catcher.
>
> Andy Pafko was at bat; the bases were full. He

hit a hot smash that was trapped by Gustine. Gustine tagged the man who was leading off third and then caught the guy coming down from second, tagged him. So he had two outs and knew there still was something but couldn't figure what—because Pafko stood stock still—never moved a step from the plate; he thought the ball had been caught. Instead it had been trapped.

Because Pafko stood still, Gustine couldn't figure out what was happening. He did a snake dance in the infield, holding the ball in his right hand, wondering what to do with it. McCullough came out and said, "Give me the ball." Gustine handed it to him, who threw to first base and tripled Pafko.

Another Pafko incident happened against St. Louis at Wrigley Field. With two out, Rocky Nelson hit a shot into left field, a sinking liner. Pafko made a diving catch—or so he thought. Umpire Al Barlick, racing out on the play, flattened his palms and said, "No, he trapped the ball." Andy in his own mind knew, and even today swears, that he caught the ball. He ran in, holding his glove high with the ball in it, heading for the bench. In the meantime Nelson continued to round the bases. Andy refused to give in. The Cubs' manager Charlie Grimm jumped up and yelled, "Andy, Andy, throw the ball! We'll argue about it later!" And with the greatest reluctance Andy fired the ball as only he could, and he hit Nelson right in the tail as he crossed home plate. And to this day, whenever they meet, Barlick and Pafko both claim they were right.

Early in his television broadcasting career Jack found himself shouting an excited "Hey, hey!" on Cubs and Sox home runs.

> When you're ad-libbing at a rate of 150 to 200 words a minute for hours at a time, you sometimes fall in love with a word or expression without realizing it. One day my crew thought they'd show me something. Hank Sauer hit a home run, and I yelled it, and the crew superimposed a great big "Hey, hey!" that covered the screen.
>
> Well, we waited for viewers' reaction. They liked it. And it is fun to have a pet expression that can be identified with you. After all, you want to react in some way to a home run; that's part of the game. Everybody yells on a home run.

In 1950 Pafko hit 36 home runs and Sauer added 32, yet the Cubs barely escaped the 1950 basement. In midseason 1951 Wrigley fired Frisch and named as player/manager Phil Cavarretta, a Cub since 1934. In 1952 the team was the surprise of the league, climbing to fifth place with a .500 record. And Sauer, dubbed "the mayor of Wrigley Field," was voted the league's Most Valuable Player.

Early in the 1953 season WGN manager Schreiber announced a multiyear agreement with Jack that made him one of the nation's highest-paid sports broadcasters. That autumn the Cubs purchased Ernie Banks, a talented twenty-two-year-old athlete, from the Kansas City Monarchs in the Negro Leagues. He had also been scouted by the White Sox, by the Cincinnati Reds, and to a lesser extent by the Yankees.

Forty years later at the annual Cubs Convention in Chicago, Jack recalled Banks's arrival: "John 'Buck' O'Neil, one of the great Negro baseball figures, was the manager of the Monarchs and a scout for the Chicago Cubs. The Negro Baseball League was very highly regarded, and once when they had a game in Sox Park, O'Neil was asked about this guy Ernie Banks. The Cubs' general manager Jim Gallagher OK'd the price, and then the Cubs agreed to sign him— scouted first at Sox Park."

Banks, also at the convention session, added his own recollection: "I joined the team in September 1953 and was just overwhelmed at Wrigley Field, walking in the park, and meeting all the players. At that time there weren't many fans, as Jack can recall, coming to the ballpark. So to be there, to walk out there, to see the vines, and see no lights, looking at the faces of all the few fans—we became friends at Wrigley Field. That's why it is called 'the friendly confines,' because it was just a friendly atmosphere for the players."

Jack quickly became a Banks fan: "Ernie was the happiest guy in the world to be in the major leagues. He was just so tickled to be playing baseball; he had a genuine love of the sport. Ernie had the ability to make a little boy or a little girl feel like the reason he came to the park that day was to see them."

Banks hit his first home run in his third Cubs game and ended the season with a .310 batting average. In spring training of 1954 the team performed poorly, and Wrigley replaced manager Cavarretta with former Cubs star Stan Hack; yet autumn brought another seventh-place finish.

In May of 1955 thirty-nine-year-old Brickhouse established a national record by telecasting his thousandth game.

WGN-TV colleagues, Cubs and White Sox officials, and American League president Will Harridge feted Jack at a celebration luncheon.

One of his "top broadcasting thrills" came at Wrigley Field later in the month. The smallest crowd of the season, fewer than three thousand, braved fifty-three-degree weather and watched Sam "Toothpick" Jones pitch a no-hit game against Pittsburgh. It was Jack's first no-hitter:

> The game bordered on the incredible. Sam, blessed with a fantastic curveball but wild most of the day, carried the drama to the hilt. This was the first no-hitter at Wrigley Field since the James Vaughn–Frederick Toney double no-hitter of 1913.
>
> In the ninth inning Sam walked the bases full of Pirates. Manager Stan Hack went to the mound and said: "Get the blankety-blank ball over the plate, or you're out of here." Then on twelve pitches Sam struck out the side—Dick Groat, Roberto Clemente, and Frank Thomas.
>
> Sam's catcher was the veteran Clyde McCullough, and that was his only no-hitter in twenty-one years of pro ball.

Jones, the first African-American player to achieve a major-league no-hitter, led the team with 14 victories (and 20 defeats). Banks's 44 home runs included 5 grand slams, a major-league record at the time. And for the rest of the decade he would average 40 homers a season.

McCullough, the last veteran of the 1945 championship team, was dropped from the roster in midseason 1956 for a young pitcher, Moe Drabowsky. The Cubs completed the season with their tenth straight year in the second division, this one in last place. Hack, once the tremendously popular third baseman who had been on all four Cubs championship teams—in 1932, 1935, 1938, and 1945—was replaced as the 1957 manager by former Cubs catcher Bob Scheffing, a season when Wrigley Field attendance dropped to its lowest in more than a decade, totaling just under 671,000.

In the mid-1950s, returning by train from announcing a Notre Dame football game, Jack learned of a college student who would become one of the best and most popular sports broadcasters in Chicago: "I was in the club car with a few friends, one of whom had a kid majoring in broadcasting at Notre Dame. I agreed to give him a tryout. He was Jack Quinlan, who became an all-time favorite of Cub fans behind the microphone. He was dynamic and authoritative, and with his sense of humor they added up to a superb announcer. Sometimes I thought you could actually hear his smile on the air."

Working first in Peoria, Quinlan was recommended by Jack in 1958 as the radio voice of the Chicago Cubs. Quinlan's color analyst was the former baseball player and manager Lou Boudreau, whom Jack describes as "the first former athlete to make it big in our broadcasting setup. I had always thought that an athlete could add to a broadcast, and Lou fit in perfectly."

The 1958 Cubs batted .265 as a team and scored 709 runs—still not enough, however, to escape their habitual second-division finish. Banks was named the league's Most Valuable Player and won *The Sporting News* Player of the Year award.

By the late 1950s significant changes were occurring in baseball. With the Dodgers and Giants relocating to California, the jet airline service that followed was a boon for scheduling and the comfort of team travel. Many players and others connected with the game, however, regretted the demise of leisurely rail travel—sportswriter Dick Young grumbling, "There's something wrong when you have to run yourself into a heart attack to catch a jet to save time."

Also, by 1959—twelve years after Jackie Robinson's rookie season—all sixteen club rosters included at least one African-American player. *Ebony* magazine reported at the time, "More than half a hundred colored players are cavorting over the big league diamonds from New York to Los Angeles, with World Series dreams riding high on the shoulders of the Negro stars."

The "zaniest" game episode Brickhouse says he ever saw came in 1959 at Wrigley Field, when two balls were in play.

Stan Musial was batting for the Cardinals. Vic Delmore was the plate umpire and Pat Pieper the Cubs' public address announcer. The Cubs had Bob Anderson pitching, Sammy Taylor catching, Tony Taylor at second, Banks playing short, with Al Dark at third. On a 3–1 pitch Anderson threw one that went over everybody's head and hit the screen. Delmore gave Musial a walk.

The Cubs loudly protested that Musial had fouled it. Pieper put the ball in his used-ball bag, but Dark—a thinking man's third baseman—ran in to snatch it from the bag. Meanwhile, Sammy Taylor by instinct accepted a new ball from Delmore. Foolishly, the Cubs didn't call time. Everybody on the Cardinals' bench yelled "Take two! Go! Go!" So, in the confusion, Musial started to steal second.

Anderson snatched the ball from the catcher and

threw way over Tony Taylor's head. At the same time, Dark threw his ball, which Banks grabbed on the shortstop side of second. They were both lousy throws. Musial saw Anderson's throw bounding wildly in the outfield and headed for third. En route, Banks tagged him with the ball Dark threw. With two balls out there, it was real confusion.

For fifteen minutes the umpires argued. They finally ruled that Dark's ball was the one in play, and Musial was out.

The Cubs finished the 1959 season in a tie for fifth place, with their best record since 1952. Banks repeated as Most Valuable Player and *The Sporting News* Player of the Year. Across town the White Sox's Nellie Fox was the American League MVP.

Charlie Grimm, Cubs manager in the 1930s and late 1940s, was once again called on, replacing Scheffing for 1960. To Jack, Grimm was "probably the best manager the team had during the time I covered them." In Grimm's thirteen years the Cubs had won three championships, but after they lost eleven of their first seventeen games in 1960, he, too, was replaced. Jack described the circumstances to Curt Smith: "Phil Wrigley called me in—this was in May—and he said, 'Jack, I want to make a trade, and I want you to take care of it.' I said, 'Oh, who's involved?' And Mr. Wrigley looked at me and said, 'I want to trade Boudreau for Grimm.' 'Boudreau for Grimm?' 'Yes,' Wrigley answered. 'Charlie's worrying himself sick over the team. He's out walking the streets when he should be resting. And between that and his coaching third base, if the Cubs don't kill him first, his sore feet will.' "

"What a team," Smith surmised: "So you went to both

guys and arranged a trade." " 'Yep,' Brickhouse said. 'A manager for a broadcaster.' Only with the Cubs."

Early in the 1960 season the Cubs acquired pitcher Don
Cardwell from the Philadelphia Phillies. Jack remembers
Cardwell's first start as a Cub: "It was on a Sunday against
the Cardinals. On that day he was as fast as any pitcher I
had covered, as fast as Bob Feller or Sandy Koufax. Cardwell threw a no-hitter, saved with two out in the ninth by
Moose Moryn's sensational shoe-top grab of Joe Cunning-
ham's sinking liner in left field. Our WGN-TV cameras watched
Wrigley Field go up for grabs!" (In late September 1995, Jack
reflected on that game after the Cubs' Frank Castillo pitched
a near no-hitter against the Cardinals. To Jack, the feat provided vivid memories of the Cardwell game. "I thought about
Moryn's great catch as I watched Sammy Sosa make a terrific dive on the St. Louis triple that broke up the ninth
inning two-out no-hitter. Sosa missed by inches. In a sense,
the Cardinals got that one back.")

In one forty-eight-hour period that summer of 1960 Jack
traveled six thousand miles for Cubs and Sox games—
Chicago to Los Angeles to Chicago to New York to Chicago. After the season Boudreau returned to broadcasting,
and since none of the managers had produced even one
winning team since 1945, Wrigley came up with an inno-
vation for 1961. He decided to rotate the coaches of his
minor-league teams and have his Cubs coaching staff rotate
as head coach. Wrigley's purpose, he said, was for better
and faster development of talent within the farm system,
and he stayed with his "college of coaches" for five seasons.

Years later Hall of Famer Lou Brock said that as a Cubs
rookie, "coming from the minors and having 14 coaches
around and you trying to please everybody can be tough on

a guy at the age I was at the time." To Jack, "The college of coaches was criticized, but on paper it had some merit. Wrigley used the system in his company, transferring managers between locations for fresh ideas. With the Cubs he felt it would provide a flow of talent from the minors to the majors."

Young outfielder Billy Williams completed the 1961 season with 25 home runs and became the first Cub voted Rookie of the Year. Teammate Ron Santo, with a .284 batting average and 23 homers, was Sophomore of the Year.

In 1962 the National League followed the American League in expanding to ten teams, with new clubs in New York and Houston. The Cubs signed Buck O'Neil as a coach, the first African-American coach in the majors. Memorable for Jack that year was his involvement in the first telecast to Europe, via the Telstar communications satellite. The July 1962 program included several American features, among them a portion of a Cubs game at Wrigley Field. He was the play-by-play announcer:

> Of course, we wanted to make a good impression. It was going to be the Cubs and Phillies on a Monday afternoon, and they didn't expect a big crowd.
>
> So, the day before, on the air I mentioned that anybody who was in uniform could come into the game the next day free of charge. We had some strange uniforms, but we got a crowd of 18,000.
>
> We had only about forty-five seconds of our game, but there was plenty of excitement. When it was time for the portion of our game to get on the air, Johnny Callison was told to go up there and swing at anything—just swing. Well, Callison hit a

pitch to George Altman in right field, and he made a pretty nice catch. At least we had some action for the people in Europe.

"We only got a brief look at the game," said a carpenter in Italy to a *Baseball Digest* reporter, "but it looked like it might be fun."

Even though Banks had another strong season, the Cubs finished in ninth place, seven games behind the expansion Houston Colt .45s (later the Astros). During the winter Wrigley reorganized his college of coaches and named veteran infielder Bob Kennedy as head coach for 1963.

During that year Jack was asked by the editors of *Chicago's American* to write a column on sports subjects. So three times weekly for several years his "Jack Brickhouse Says" appeared in the sports section. "I took a portable typewriter on the road. One time between Washington and Baltimore, I hired a limousine and sat in the backseat typing the column to meet their deadline. A lot of times I would write in the hotel room. There was only one that I didn't do myself. I was detained somewhere and couldn't make the deadline, so Jack Rosenberg wrote it for me."

One day in July of 1963, WGN-TV carried the Cubs and the White Sox games simultaneously on a split screen. The station alternated Vince Lloyd's play-by-play from Comiskey Park with Brickhouse at Wrigley Field: "We cut back and forth from one game to another and didn't miss a run or a key play. The communication and instantaneous switching procedures were so smooth it was almost unbelievable— thanks to about fifty dedicated people behind the scenes."

The Cubs' 1963 record of 87–74 was their best in seventeen years, yet they finished in seventh place. Prior to the

1964 season Jack was elected to the Cubs' board of directors, a move that was approved in advance by the White Sox owners. He held the board position until 1975, then tendered his resignation after a question arose over potential conflict-of-interest issues between Wrigley ownership and WGN broadcasting contracts.

In June 1964 the Cubs dealt outfielder Brock to St. Louis in a six-player trade that also included Cardinals pitcher Ernie Broglio—generally considered the worst trade in Cubs history. Brock went on to hit .348 and led the Cardinals to the pennant, while the sore-armed Broglio won a mere seven games for the Cubs. To many fans the trade haunted their team for years.

Cubs spring training in 1965 was interrupted by tragedy. WGN broadcaster Jack Quinlan, driving to the Mesa, Arizona, training site, was killed when his car skidded into a semitrailer truck. Brickhouse and the team were devastated. He offered Vince Lloyd the choice between continuing on television and taking Quinlan's job. Lloyd decided to join Boudreau on the radio, and Jack then teamed with Lloyd Pettit, "one of the most gifted play-by-play men I have ever known. He did baseball, football, and of course hockey. Nobody has ever done hockey better than Lloyd."

One of the very few baseball events that eluded Brickhouse in his career was broadcasting a perfect game—although with the 1958 Sox and 1972 Cubs he announced games that came within a single out of the accomplishment: "The Cubs were involved in one at Los Angeles on September 9, 1965. The Dodgers' Sandy Koufax was letter perfect, striking out fourteen batters. Bob Hendley, the Cubs' pitcher, allowed only one hit in the 1–0 loss. WGN Television didn't carry the game. Vince Lloyd and Lou Boudreau experienced the thrill of doing it on WGN Radio and, I might add, did themselves proud with a memorable job."

After the 1965 season Wrigley gave up on his college of coaches and signed longtime player and successful manager Leo Durocher to lead the Cubs. Durocher was an entertaining personality, providing the media with frequent one-liners and discourses that helped rekindle interest in the lagging team: "I'm here to find out why the Cubs are an eighth-place team" and "If some of my players want to stay out late, all they have to do is call me and I'll join 'em."

Early the following season Durocher made a fortunate trade for pitcher Ferguson Jenkins, who debuted with six shutout innings and a home run. Several other Cubs—especially Santo and Glenn Beckert—had successful seasons, yet the team tumbled to last place. Equaling their 1962 worst-ever record of 59–103, the Cubs allowed the expansion New York Mets their first escape from the basement.

Then, in mid-1967, with Jack in his last year of broadcasting both the Cubs and the Sox, both teams were in the thick of pennant races. Under Durocher the Cubs were climbing from last place, while the Sox were continuing their first-division status. Jack reveled in it, telling Bill Irvin of *Chicago's American*:

> It's a wonderful feeling. . . . We have a tendency to get a little excited anyway, as broadcasters, but now we find ourselves getting carried away more than usual. And I've never known mail like this. It's fantastic. I've put on extra help to handle it. I have a policy in which I insist on seeing every letter that comes in, even tho [sic] I may not be the one to answer it, but I'll see it. You can't use a form letter answer to this kind of mail. . . .
>
> This is the first year I've gotten mail from

overseas, not only from fellows in the service, and in Viet Nam, but from Chicago tourists who are picking up overseas editions of American newspapers and sending me the clippings with notes attached, "Here we are in London" or "Here we are in Paris." When you're that far from home and a Cub fan and you read about what's happening you can't resist the temptation to sit down to write to somebody. I guess they feel that I'm the link.

During the Cubs' winning string a rating service recorded approximately 1.5 million WGN viewers of a Cubs-Cardinals game in St. Louis—an amazing 46 percent audience share. On the following night the viewer numbers were double those of the first game. With Santo at third base, Don Kessinger at shortstop, Beckert at second, and Banks at first, the 1967 Cubs—for the first time in twenty-two years—led the league in fielding. The team finished in third place.

From the time in 1948 when both Chicago teams had begun televising their games, the owners honored a "handshake agreement" not to televise away games when one team was at home. In 1967, after Sox owner Arthur Allyn left WGN for WFLD and decided to have all Sox games televised, Wrigley gave WGN permission to cover the Cubs' entire schedule. And Jack covered the Cubs exclusively, still with "that boyish enthusiasm that nothing could seem to shake," according to Rosenberg. "He was just as excited in the ninth inning of the second game of a doubleheader as in the first inning of the first game. Didn't matter whether the team was in first place or the cellar. After five or six hours of broadcasting, he'd just be catching his second wind."

Finally up from two decades in the second division, the Cubs under Durocher recorded three second-place and two third-place finishes from 1968 to 1972. The closest race came in 1969, when for 154 games the team held the Eastern Division lead in the expanded twelve-team league. Jack described an August game against the Atlanta Braves, pitched by the Cubs' left-hander Ken Holtzman, as "the most interesting no-hitter I've ever seen, because he did it without any strikeouts. In the seventh inning Hank Aaron slammed a towering fly ball to left. I yelled, 'And there goes the no-hitter!' Boy, was I glad I was wrong. The ball hung over Waveland Avenue for an instant, but a strong north wind blew it back into Billy Williams's glove in left at the curvature in the wall. The last guy Holtzman faced in that game was also Aaron. And Kenny went right to him, on a full count got him to ground out to Beckert at second base—none of that trying to 'pitch around him' business."

Late in the season the team was still in first place. Cubs fans were wild for a long-awaited championship, only to encounter sore disappointment when the team fell into a final-stretch tailspin. Jack thought that the Cubs "were a cinch that year, I really did. I was taken in by it. Until then I had never been involved with a club that was that far ahead. I didn't envision the Mets being good enough to go out and win 29 of their last 37 or some silly figure like that."

Those "Amazin' Mets"—the long-hapless New York team—rose from ninth place in 1968, putting on a furious late charge to capture the National League Eastern Division title by eight games. The Cubs finished second with a 92–70 record, their best since the 1945 pennant year. After the season a disappointed Brickhouse discussed the situation with his *Peoria Journal-Star* friend Paul King.

> The Cubs were an awfully tired team down the stretch. Hindsight is a fine thing, but it's too bad that the Cub regulars weren't able to be rested more near the end of the season.

> Don Kessinger was so tired he could hardly
> lift his bat. Glenn Beckert was the same way.
> Randy Hundley was just a shell of what he'd been
> earlier. Then we had Ron Santo, Jim Hickman and
> Billy Williams playing with injuries.

Throughout his career the genial Brickhouse had only one professional quarrel that went even partly public. It was with Leo Durocher and happened while he was the Cubs' manager.

> Leo always felt that *Chicago's American* sportswriter
> Jim Enright and I were trying to run him out of
> town. I don't like to bear grudges, but I helped Leo
> get the job in Chicago, got him a WGN radio-televi-
> sion package and advance money—he should have
> been grateful for that alone. But he resented Banks
> and me. And the way he treated Banks was brutal,
> one of the cruelest things I've ever seen. Leo hated
> to share the spotlight, and he took it out on Banks,
> and some of that jealousy was directed at me.
>
> Durocher was personally more responsible for
> the Cubs' collapse in 1969 than any other person. He
> panicked. He didn't handle the ball club correctly
> when the pennant was on the line. He stopped man-
> aging. In the end Chicago was just not his town.
> There's a lot of sadness to his story with the Cubs.

The feud was reportedly repaired prior to the 1970 season. At spring training in Arizona the two, "who didn't speak to each other the last half of the 1969 season," according to *The Sporting News*, "were closeted in Durocher's office" for a half hour, then went on the air together for an interview session.

With a small Wrigley Field crowd on Senior Citizens Day
in May 1970, Jack was at the microphone for another memorable occasion: two out in the second inning, Ernie Banks
at the plate, and the Atlanta Braves' Pat Jarvis on the mound.
Jack gave this play-by-play:

> One-one pitch. He swings and a drive—a liner,
> left field! It's—Hey! Hey! There it is! On your feet,
> everybody—this is it! Mr. Banks has just hit his
> 500th career homer! He is getting a standing ova-
> tion! He is trotting to third base! A handshake
> from Peanuts Lowrey. He hit a low liner—a fast-
> ball. Doffs his cap as he steps on home plate! . . .
> Waves to the fans as he jogs into that dugout! They
> are standing here at Wrigley Field and giving Ernie
> an ovation!

Then in the ninth inning Banks's teammate and longtime
friend Billy Williams homered to tie the game, and Santo won
it with a bases-loaded single. "There was no way we were
going to lose that game and spoil Ernie's day for him," said
Williams, who later in the season set a league record of
1,117 consecutive game appearances.

During 1970 former Yankees slugger Joe Pepitone joined
the Cubs. To Jack,

> Joe was a real sweet guy, and he had a lot of clown
> in him. He should have been the Yankees' successor
> to Mickey Mantle or Joe DiMaggio, but it didn't
> work out.
>   Joey Amalfitano was the Cubs' first-base coach
> and in Pepitone's first day with the ball club said to
> him, "Look, if you get on first base and Leo crosses

his legs in the dugout, the hit and run sign is on."
Sure enough, a few innings later, Pepitone got on first
base. Joey was coaching at first, and Pepitone took a
good lead. Then Durocher crossed his legs in the
dugout, so the hit and run was on. Amalfitano, want-
ing to make sure that Pepitone caught the sign,
winked at him. Pepitone winked back, blew him a
kiss—and got picked off first base!

With Pepitone's 27 home runs, the Cubs' 1970 total was
179—3 under the club record. In 1971 the team had three
players—Banks, Williams, and Santo—with 300 or more
career home runs. Holtzman pitched his second no-hitter;
Jenkins won 24 games, hit 6 home runs, and won the Cy
Young Award, the first Cub so honored. Banks retired at the
end of the season, then in 1977—his first year of eligibility—
was elected to the National Baseball Hall of Fame. He and
Jack have been longtime friends and golfing buddies. "Ernie
is the most popular, most successful single competitive performer in the history of Chicago sports. Here's a guy with
512 home runs, Most Valuable Player with two losers (1958
and 1959), and is probably as good an ambassador outside
the ballpark as the sport has ever known."

An entertaining assignment for Jack came in 1971, narrating a bestselling record album, *Great Moments in Cubs
Baseball!*—play-by-play highlights from radio broadcasts
beginning in the 1930s. About the same time a "dump
Durocher" clique was forming in Chicago, as animosity
increased between him and some of the players. He charged
that the "Unholy Six," led by Brickhouse and Enright and
including other sportswriters, were "out to get him." After
the 1972 All-Star break, Durocher left the Cubs, and former

Giants outfielder Whitey Lockman replaced him for the rest
of the season. A pennant-winning manager with both the
Giants and the Dodgers, Durocher later stated, "I'm always
associated with New York, but I think the years I put in with
the Cubs were some of my best. It's always harder to start
with an inexperienced team than it is to start with proven
winners. . . . I enjoyed those Chicago teams." In his 1975
autobiography, however, Durocher still had only unkind
words for both Brickhouse and Enright.

For Jack, one of his "big thrills—if not the biggest" was
a second Wrigley Field no-hitter of the 1972 season. The first,
by Burt Hooton, was a 4–0 win over Philadelphia in mid-
April. The other was by Milt Pappas in September.

> Pappas came within one pitch of a perfect game.
> With two out in the ninth, he had a two-and-two
> count on San Diego pinch hitter Larry Stahl, and
> home plate umpire Bruce Froemming called a close
> low pitch ball three. Then, with a full count, he called
> a fourth ball, ruining the perfect game. Pappas was
> the first man I've ever seen who threw a no-hitter but
> was steaming. He went on to get the last out and
> win 8–0.
>
> The next day at the ballpark Pappas said to
> Froemming, "You know in your heart that was a
> strike. Just think, both of us would have been famous.
> There are only a few umpires to call a perfect game,
> and you would have been added to the list."
>
> Froemming said, "Milt, if I had called either of
> those a strike, I wouldn't be able to live with myself";
> whereupon Pappas answered, "Then how do you live
> with yourself on all of those other lousy calls you
> make?"

When the season ended, the Cubs were in second place. Williams's .333 batting average was the highest in both leagues, and Jenkins became the first pitcher with six consecutive twenty-game seasons. During the following year, 1973, hopes were high for a winning team; at the beginning of July the Cubs held first place by eight games. Then a collapse greater than in 1969 tumbled them to fifth place. Lockman was replaced by rookie manager Jim Marshall, but the team was even worse in 1974—dropping to the cellar.

In 1975 Bill Madlock, replacing Santo at third base, led the league with a .354 batting average—the highest by a Cub in thirty years. And the team finished in fifth place; the beginning of a tenuous five-year stay in the first division. Madlock won his second consecutive batting title in 1976; Jose Cardenal was the top Cubs base stealer, and Rick Monday led the team in home runs. During the winter Kennedy was brought back as general manager, and he named Cubs coach Herman Franks as his new field boss.

On April 12, 1977, owner Philip Wrigley died, leaving the team to his son, William. That year the *Tribune* reported Brickhouse as Chicago's third-highest-paid television broadcaster, earning $150,000 annually. The Cubs led the league for sixty-nine days and had a twenty-game winner in Rick Reuschel. Bruce Sutter finished with 31 saves and an amazing 1.35 ERA, but the team finished fourth, with an 81–81 record.

In 1978 the Cubs climbed to third place, and Bill Buckner, obtained from the Dodgers for Monday, was the team's leading hitter. Sutter contributed 27 saves, but the season record was a disappointing 79–83.

On August 5, 1979, Jack announced his 5,000th baseball game for WGN (4,650 on television). After the first game of a Sunday Cubs-Cardinals doubleheader, he received plaudits from Chicago mayor Jane Byrne and Illinois governor James R. Thompson. Even the *Tribune*'s editorial page editor recognized the feat: "Brickhouse has become almost as well established an institution since he broadcast his first ballgame for WGN in 1940 as if he had been around for 5,000 years."

His team finished 1979 in fifth place. First baseman Dave Kingman, with 48 home runs, became the third Cub in the decade to win the league batting title. Sutter won the Cy Young Award with 37 saves. A week before the season ended, Franks had resigned, and veteran coach Preston Gomez took over as manager for 1980.

He, too, struggled with the team and in August, after ninety games, was replaced by coach Amalfitano. Buckner succeeded an injured Kingman as the league batting champion, and Sutter again led the league in saves. But the Cubs reverted to their mid-1960s form, finishing last in the division with the worst record in the league, 64–98.

In 1981 the Wrigley family's long ownership of the Chicago Cubs ended with its purchase by the Tribune Company. Like most fans, Jack viewed the sale as ensuring survival for the north-side team. "I had to think Bill Wrigley felt that way about it. And he sold it to a substantial organization that he knew would keep the club in Chicago."

That was also Jack's final season as the Cubs' broadcaster, a decision he and the team management had reached two years earlier. The schedule was marred in midseason by a players' strike, giving Jack his first nonworking Fourth of July in forty-seven years. On the strike he said to a reporter for the *Glencoe News*, "I was wrong on every turn on this thing. I couldn't conceive of adult minds being that stupid that they'd let this happen. Once it did happen, I was convinced it couldn't last more than 24 or 48 hours. So I was 0-for-2."

The longest professional sports strike to that time ended after seven weeks, and Jack resumed his play-by-play. The Cubs struggled in the second division on their way to an encore in the cellar, prompting Kingman to remark, "There's nothing wrong with this team that more pitching, more fielding, and more hitting couldn't help."

In late September, *Chicago Tribune* columnist Bob Verdi reported on both Jack's imminent departure from the broadcasting booth and yet another Cubs loss.

> When the Cubs were stinking up Montreal beyond the call of duty last week, a tougher voice might have bludgeoned them. Jack's stiletto was gentle. Observing the 11–0 seance was, he said, like watching the married guys play the single guys in the company softball game.
>
> Jack Brickhouse is merely what all of us who take ourselves too seriously would like to be, but can't be. He's gee whiz when the rest of us are going aw, nuts, in a business that unduly bloats egos and tends to render its balloon-headed stars larger than the events they cover. Jack Brickhouse still has the time and sincere inclination to trade handshakes and an old story with the elevator operator. . . .
>
> "I've debated Howard Cosell about this 'tell-it-like-it-is' stuff," says Brickhouse. "I told him he's got his act, I've got mine. . . . All this personal stuff about athletes' lives. I started in an era when you couldn't even mention homosexuality or pregnancy on the air. There's still a little of that in me about what's right for a broadcast. I don't want to be a stick-in-the-mud, but when you go overboard, you don't hurt the athlete only. You hurt his wife going to the grocery store, his kid going to school. Why? What does it prove?" . . .

"I've done more TV baseball than any broadcaster ever," he says, "and I'd be lying if I said
that every day, I couldn't wait to get to the ballpark. But whenever I wasn't up, I'd open a letter
from some shut-in or look behind home plate at
all those people in wheelchairs. If, somehow, I
helped provide an escape, then maybe I did a
decent job."

Jack's final home game was celebrated by scores of fans,
and he told one of the many reporters: "You know, it's great
to see a crowd that size happy. That's something we can use
more of these days." After the game, "TV stations were following me downstairs into the Pink Poodle, the Wrigley Field
lunch room. It was quite an emotional scene. I was besieged
for autographs by young and old alike. On my way to the
Poodle, I was summoned by what must have been a thousand fans outside, to stick my head out of the Poodle and
take one more bow. What a feeling. I'll never forget that
moment!"

As his replacement Jack had groomed broadcast veteran
Milo Hamilton, switching announcing roles for the second
half of the season. In November, Hamilton was surprised and
bitterly disappointed when the new Cubs owners announced
that they had signed Harry Caray for the job. The *Tribune*
reported that "after a flurry of introductions Brickhouse was
presented to bring Caray—his successor—in from the
wings." The two had been colleagues in baseball since 1945
and in Chicago for the ten years that Caray was the White
Sox broadcaster.

But at age sixty-five, Brickhouse wasn't ready to retire.
He "just went back to his radio roots" on WGN several days
a week with sports programs and interviews with Cubs fans.
When the team closed in on the Eastern Division title in 1984,

Jack told the *Sun-Times*' Herb Gould: "I'd be an awful liar if I said I didn't want to come back and do a couple of innings just for old time's sake. But I'd like to have that be their biggest problem. At this point, I'll settle for two good seats."

He was, to no one's surprise, invited to the broadcast booth during the divisional playoffs, which the Cubs—true to the Billy Goat hex—lost to the San Diego Padres. In 1988 the Cubs broke the St. Louis Browns' record of forty-three consecutive seasons without winning a league championship. (After 1995 the Cubs' record was fifty straight seasons.)

Jack has returned to the Wrigley Field broadcast booth on several occasions, including its dedication in his honor in 1982 and the first game played under the new lights in 1988. For that occasion Joe Mantegna wrote in the *New York Times*, "To a true Cub fan, all the tangible symbols of devotion—the ivy-covered wall, Brickhouse's 'Hey, Hey!' Ernie Banks, Harry Caray's rendition of 'Take Me Out to the Ballgame,' and all the rest—were always joined by that one intangible: the lack of lights. Well, scratch the intangible."

Jack participates in the hugely successful annual Cubs convention. Held in midwinter at a downtown Chicago hotel, the conventions attract zealous fans for the program sessions, autograph opportunities, memorabilia purchases, and chance conversations with their heroes. In addition to graciously signing autographs and visiting with fans, Jack convenes a program with Cubs Hall of Fame players. The 1993 session was especially memorable, as described by the *Tribune*'s Mike Conklin:

> It was the most poignant moment in eight years for the Cubs' annual convention. Ferguson Jenkins, making his initial public appearance since the tragic death of his girlfriend and daughter last month, was part of a Hall of Fame panel with

emcee Jack Brickhouse and former teammates Billy
Williams and Ernie Banks. In his first response to
a question from Brickhouse, Jenkins told the
hushed, Grand Ballroom SRO crowd in the Hilton
& Towers what it felt like when he was named to
baseball's hall.

Noting that it occurred in the few days
between the time his wife, Mary Anne, was
injured and then died from an automobile acci-
dent in 1991, Fergie said, "When I told her, it was
the last time she smiled." Jenkins, starting to get
misty-eyed, concluded: "To this day, I don't know
what I said at the induction [in Cooperstown]. My
18 years as a player went so quickly, and now I'm
going to be 50."

His answer was met with polite applause that
grew and grew. Finally, after a minute, the several
thousand spectators were all on their feet with a
full-bore, emotional standing ovation. Fergie took
off his glasses, wiped his eyes, got up from his
chair and retreated to the curtain behind the stage
to regain his composure. "He'll be back," Brickhouse said. A few minutes later, the ex-Cub did
return to his seat and the program continued.

At the 1995 convention Jack was a panelist with Vince
Lloyd, Lou Brock, and Ernie Broglio, discussing "The
Trade"—the 1964 swap of second-year Cubs outfielder Brock
for established St. Louis pitcher Broglio. Within two years
Broglio would be out of baseball, while Brock went on to a
Hall of Fame career with the Cardinals. Jack set the stage
for their discussion:

> The trade wasn't a bombshell at the time. June 15,
> 1964—just the June 15 trading deadline—a deal
> between the Cardinals and the Cubs. The Cubs

needed pitching; the Cardinals needed young ballplayers with some hitting and offensive ability.

The deal was Ernie Broglio, along with Doug Clemmons and Bobby Shantz, the little left-handed pitcher, in exchange for a kid named Lou Brock, Jack Spring, and Paul Toth, pitchers. I'll tell you something: if you check the records, you'll find that the media in Chicago and in St. Louis were interesting. The Cubs media were absolutely in favor of the trade—no criticism whatsoever. The Cardinals media were really burned up.

When the Cubs got Broglio, he was only twenty-eight years old and had won 67 ballgames, lost only 50. They got a terrific proven player for a young kid with a lot of promise but hadn't guaranteed anything—at a time the Cubs needed pitching very badly.

Brock remembered his relief that he wasn't "headed for Wenatchee, Washington, in the minors. I was told, 'You've been traded for Ernie Broglio.' 'Ernie Broglio? He's a twenty-game winner.' I began to perk up a little, thinking, I've got stock, I've got value!"

Broglio responded: "You talk about stock? I went from a case of Budweiser to a pack of Wrigley's spearmint!" Two years after the trade, a calcium condition in his arm ended Broglio's baseball career. He described his last day:

> I was going to pitch the second game against the Mets. In those days, if you had one arm and one leg, you still wanted to go out there and pitch against the Mets.
>
> I was rooming with Joey Amalfitano. That Sunday morning we were getting ready to go to church, and my elbow just froze on me. I said, "Joe, I cannot move. I can't do anything." He said,

"What's wrong?" I said, "It's locked." He throws me the room key to the hotel and says "Here, unlock the son of a bitch." I said, "This is serious!" He took me to the Mets organization, who gave me a shot of cortisone and put me on a plane back to Chicago.

A fan observed that "the fateful trade made a big difference for where we were in 1968 and 1969. We might have had a championship team." Jack agreed, but he added, "Every ball club has had trades like that one. After all, you're dealing with human beings."

Among the celebrities at the Cubs' conventions and other fan gatherings, Jack remains a favorite. In a recent book on the Cubs he is described as being as famous and popular "as any of the players."

The author Curt Smith included Jack in his testimony to the baseball broadcasters of the 1950s and 1960s, "future Hall of Famers, institutions, and household words . . . they sketched every game through paint-by-number. Were you a thousand miles from the monuments at Yankee Stadium, or the ivy at Wrigley Field, more fragrant and spectacular each year? . . . No, you weren't; you were *there*. Your radio and television became the brush. . . . These announcers were not giants, exactly or even only, but as friends are around the dinner table, almost family."

CHAPTER 7

Wrestling, Boxing, Bears, and Bulls

I N 1948, THE BREAKTHROUGH YEAR IN CHICAGO TELEVI-
sion, Brickhouse began a sports association that was to
last for nearly a decade. Frank Schreiber assigned him to
broadcast professional wrestling for WGN-TV and the DuMont
Network. Jack strongly protested the assignment, arguing
that he was a professional announcer and that wrestling was
a phony gimmick—"hippodrome, not a sport at all."

Losing the argument and "doing what I was darned
well told," Jack for nine years telecast weekly wrestling
matches from three Chicago locations: Marigold Gardens,
on the north side; Madison Arena, on the west side; and
Midway Arena, on the south side. He soon came to like the
assignments.

Wrestling grew as a television feature, with station
after station joining our network from the Marigold.
The bonanza spread eastward, and wrestling names
became household words.

Wrestling fans are a cult, and wrestling was a vital part of television in the late '40s. We used to say there were two kinds of people, those who watched wrestling on television and those who wouldn't admit it. Also, it didn't take me long to discover that professional wrestling was theatrical rather than phony.

Probably the most popular wrestler of the era was Verne Gagne, a handsome Norwegian. To Jack,

Gagne and wrestling were made for each other. He had played football at the University of Minnesota, and he won four Big Ten collegiate wrestling championships. I recall his first pro match in Chicago opposite the champion, Lou Thesz. Fred Kohler, who was Gagne's promoter and undoubtedly the best promoter ever, predicted: "If he makes any kind of showing against Thesz on television tonight, Gagne will become one of the great ones." After the wrestlers fought to a one-hour draw, he was an overnight sensation.

I was the ring announcer when Gagne made his first appearance at Madison Square Garden. Before the match I checked on two previous events. The New York Rangers and Boston Bruins game had about fifty-five hundred fans; a boxing match between Teddy "Red Top" Davis and Georgie Araujo drew somewhere around forty-nine hundred. For wrestling the Garden had been getting crowds of three thousand to four thousand. The night we were there, a capacity of some seventeen thousand fans

showed up. They came from Connecticut, Pennsylvania, Massachusetts, New Jersey, upstate New
York—all over. We had to have a police escort. It was
terribly exciting.

In my mind, even now, Verne Gagne remains a
superstar in the world of wrestling, the sport's most
successful figure, yet a man completely unaffected by
his great accomplishments.

Among the outlandish showmen of the wrestling circuit
was "The Mighty Atlas." Morris Shapiro, according to Jack
in *Thanks for Listening!*, "advertised himself as wrestling's
strongest man. He could very well have been just that. The
mighty Atlas had gimmicks. He would tie one end of a rope
to a car bumper, put the other end of the rope in his mouth
and pull the car down the street of a small town in order to
build up the gate that night."

In 1951 *Tribune* reporter Anton Remenih wrote about the
sport's increasing popularity. "Wrestling is unique in the
entertainment field because no rehearsals are held before the
curtain goes up. There just isn't time. Groaners travel from
town to town on one night stands. . . . Above all, wrestling
is a business—big business now, thanks to television." Remenih asked Jack to comment on the frequent allegation of
fixed matches. His response: "Whether matches are set up
is really beside the point as far as the televiewing fan is concerned. The great appeal is the realism. There is still nothing phony about a cracked skull or leg. The injury rate in
this business is terrific." He later commented that "tele-
viewers must enjoy wrestling matches, because wherever a
station has dropped the weekly program the protests have

been so numerous that the matches have been restored."

By 1955 Jack was described as the "coast-to-coast voice of wrestling." He had broadcast more than one hundred championship defenses by Gagne and at least fifty wins by Buddy Rogers, described by Jack as "a handsome blond crowd pleaser." Once a New York journalist asked the *Chicago Tribune*'s Dave Condon to arrange an interview with Brickhouse. "My editors tell me," explained the writer, "that I can't do an article without talking with Brickhouse because he is synonymous with wrestling." And an Albany, New York, reporter covered his appearances there: "Living room spectators have come to accept Brickhouse as part of the wrestling picture—and with his six foot, three inch frame, he does carry the heft of a good many grapplers. From New York through Chicago, in more than 200 communities, he is identified with the Saturday night DuMont network shows out of Marigold Gardens as if he were a main eventer himself."

A columnist for the *New York Post* noted that Jack interviewed wrestlers "with a respect usually reserved for clergymen." And in Syracuse he was described as "one of the really first-rate guys in the sports business. . . . He's almost the celebrated figure that Verne Gagne is for the mat fans." Syndicated New York reporter Dan Parker, however, cautioned wrestling fans on the "quasi-sport . . . histrionics," adding that every Saturday evening Brickhouse was on the television screen with "straight-faced commentaries on the patent but harmless pretending of the heroes and villains. . . . As a salesman for The Game, Brickhouse has no equal. Whenever he is introduced at a wrestling show here, he is cheered like a fellow who has announced he will give away $100 bills to all comers."

Jack relishes the memories of wrestling's heyday some forty years ago. "You got a dollar's worth of entertainment for your dollar, and I defy football, baseball, or any of the rest to match that. Over the years I encountered many old-timers who were unaware that I broadcast baseball and football and knew me only for my work on wrestling."

Another sport for which Brickhouse received national assignments was boxing. In Peoria he had acquired considerable experience covering boxing contests, especially the Golden Gloves bouts he broadcast on radio three nights a week. From Chicago Stadium he continued with Golden Gloves coverage on both radio and television and in 1946 began announcing professional boxing on the CBS radio network. In September 1950 he and Russ Hodges were in New York to broadcast the heavyweight championship fight between Joe Louis, coming out of retirement, and Ezzard "Quiet Tiger" Charles. Although the fifteen-round contest drew only twenty-two thousand fans to Yankee Stadium, the radio and television audience was estimated at more than twenty-five million. Louis lost by decision, then soon retired again.

The following March, Brickhouse teamed with Jack Drees on CBS in Detroit for a heavyweight championship bout between Charles and challenger Jersey Joe Walcott. Charles retained the title in a fight that sportswriter Dan Parker described as "colorless mediocrity." But he complimented the broadcast coverage:

> Radio listeners can thank Jack Brickhouse for a calm, truthful word picture of the bout. Jack seldom raised his voice above conversational pitch

and when he did, you knew it was because the
action warranted it. On the other hand, he never
hesitated to tell his listeners when the fighters were
clinching or just gaping at each other. The first
commandment of blow-by-blow fight announcers
has always been: "Thou shalt make the fight seem
like the second battle of the Marne even though
it be but a game of ring-around-the-rosy." Brickhouse is to be commended for his devotion to the
truth.

Writing for *Chicago's American* a decade later, Jack
recalled the assignment:

> I was broadcasting on radio and at the same time
> was acutely aware that some people might turn
> down the TV sound and watch while listening to
> radio. . . .
>   It turned out to be one of the great waltzes of
> all time. Walcott continually forced clinches open-
> ing up for a little flurry at the finish of each stanza.
> Charles won the 15-round decision in one of the
> dullest fights ever staged.
>   It sounded that way on the broadcast too, and
> I knew there would be a stormy meeting with the
> sponsor and advertising agency Monday morning
> [in New York].
>   I went in armed with newspaper reports roast-
> ing the show. I was especially pleased to have the
> famous syndicated columns of Dan Parker and Bill
> Corum, who really made hamburger of the thing.
> The sponsor's complaint was, "Why did you have
> to knock it so much?"
>   My argument: "Because it was a lousy fight
> and I wasn't about to call it anything else with all
> those TV sets on. Look what the newspapers

wrote. Look here at the columns of Parker and Corum for instance!"

This turned out to be the weakest card I could play. The chief huckster trumped my ace with a beaut. "Jack, perhaps you don't know this but Mr. Parker is in Phoenix and Mr. Corum is in Florida. The TV cable hasn't reached these markets yet. Both men covered the fight by listening to your broadcast!"

The agency manager then gave Jack another chance. "You're working Bratton-Fusari next week, so see what you can do on that one. Try to find some positives, Jack."

On March 15, 1951, Johnny Bratton fought Charley Fusari at Chicago Stadium for the vacant world welterweight championship. To Jack, "it was one of the great fights of all time—fifteen great rounds of broadcasting." Afterward the New York agency offered him a long-term announcing contract. "But they were the agency for Pabst Brewery, and in Chicago our baseball games were sponsored by Hamm's Beer. It would have been a major conflict. I gave up boxing broadcasts, and then Jack Drees became a very popular fight announcer."

Brickhouse continued to cover boxing for his radio and television sports programs. In 1946 popular Chicago middleweight Tony Zale had won the championship from Rocky Graziano. In 1947 Jack was at Chicago Stadium for the return match, which "broke the gate record for an indoor fight—better than $400,000." In the grueling fight Zale closed one of Graziano's eyes and nearly closed the other. But Jack remembers, "The referee, Johnny Behr, had the unfortunate responsibility of taking the title from Zale while he was still standing. The 120-degree heat under the ring lights got to him." After regaining the championship, an elated Graziano called out his memorable "Hey, Ma . . . I told you somebody up there likes me!"

In 1951 Jack was at Chicago Stadium when Sugar Ray Robinson knocked out Jake LaMotta to win the middleweight championship. "Sugar Ray just had too many guns. LaMotta got up from the canvas, looked at the crowd, and asked, 'What else could I do? I did my best.' "

In the spring of 1953 Jack saw another Walcott performance, his fight with Rocky Marciano for the heavyweight title. Only a few months earlier Marciano had delivered a thirteenth-round knockout punch to Walcott in the first "pay-per-view" closed-circuit telecast. The return bout was at Chicago Stadium, and, according to the *Tribune*, Walcott angered the crowd "by going down and out in the first round before either fighter breaks a sweat." Jack recalls, "That fight was over almost before we got to our seats. Afterward I called for the film and looked at it a dozen times. I was convinced that Jersey Joe could have gotten back into the fight. At the referee's count of ten Joe jumped up like a high school actor flubbing his lines. He never intended to continue."

A decade later Jack was at Comiskey Park to report on the heavyweight championship fight between Charles "Sonny" Liston and Floyd Patterson. Patterson was knocked out in two minutes of the first round and left the stadium wearing eyeglasses and a phony beard disguise. Jack "really felt sorry for him; Liston was such a bully."

In 1967 Jack was among the participants at a tribute to 1930s boxer Barney Ross:

> Barney was a friend. I had covered some of his fights; he was an outstanding lightweight and welterweight

champion. When World War II came along, he went into the Marine Corps. He won the Silver Star because on guard duty one night on Guadalcanal he killed twenty-two Japanese soldiers and consequently saved his group from being wiped out.

Wounded and suffering from malaria, he came back to Chicago before the war was over. There was a huge civic celebration welcoming him home. We did a WGN radio broadcast, beginning with his arrival at Midway Airport.

Because of the malaria, Barney became addicted to the drugs used in his treatment. That began what he called his "toughest fight." He voluntarily entered a federal hospital in Kentucky and managed to win that battle.

After he contracted throat cancer, we held a benefit for him, organized by his friend Ira Colitz. Boxing champions Tony Zale and Ezzard Charles were both there.

Barney was a remarkable example of how to fight against odds. He was wounded, afflicted with malaria, and later cancer—yet he took them all on. Just like he had won his boxing titles.

In 1953 Jack added professional football to his radio sports schedule. He replaced broadcaster Bert Wilson, teaming with *Sun-Times* columnist Irv Kupcinet for nearly a quarter of a century with the Chicago Bears on WGN.

Kup to me was an ideal partner for Bears' football. He had played the game in college and briefly as a pro. He had been an NFL official. And he gave the broadcasts a certain celebrity status.

I'll never forget a Bears game against the Rams at the Los Angeles Coliseum, the first year we were together. For his interviews at halftime I asked Kup, "Would you like for me to help line up some people? I know quite a few out here." He said he didn't need any help, and that was a real understatement.

Halftime came, and I turned over the microphone to Kup. His first guest was Carmen Basilio, fresh from his welterweight championship win over Sugar Ray Robinson. Basilio was the hottest name in boxing at that time. When he finished, Bob Hope walked in—at the height of his career. And when Harry Truman came to the booth and asked "Where's Kup?" I knew this guy didn't need my help.

For Jack, reporting the Bears games was "exciting from the start. Our first game, in 1953, was against the new Baltimore team. A Colts player, Bert Rechichar, kicked a fifty-six-yard field goal. He wasn't even the regular kicker!"

The Bears of 1953 lost eight games, their worst season since 1929. In 1954 the team began a three-year winning record, but George Halas, their head coach since 1946, retired after the 1955 season.

Kupcinet, in his book *Kup's Chicago*, wrote of his broadcasting partner: "As his winter afternoon radio programs with disk jockey Eddie Hubbard demonstrate, Jack Brickhouse is quite a guy. Just when listeners expect him to discuss baseball, football, wrestling, or one of his other sports specialties, he'll launch into an informed discourse on something like the price of tea in Tahiti. Particularly amusing are his stories of his early radio experiences."

With a 9–2–1 record in 1956, the Bears met the New

York Giants at Yankee Stadium for the National Football
League championship. Jack was selected for this first nationally televised championship game:

> My NBC partner was Red Grange. He handled the
> color and analysis, and I did the play-by-play. Our
> broadcast booth was in a far corner of Yankee Sta-
> dium, under the stands and completely exposed to
> wind and cold and noise of the fans. We couldn't even
> see the scoreboard, and we had to make a phone call
> to find out the time remaining.
>
> It was so cold that the spotters couldn't work. I
> could feel the chill in my nose and eyes and mouth
> as I talked.
>
> The Giants won the championship, 47–7. In their
> dressing room after the game the players were excited
> about their great defensive line and the clutch pass-
> ing, receiving, and running. New York hadn't won a
> title since 1938, and they glowed in the heat of the
> win.
>
> But the Bears didn't glow. They were just frozen.

After a disappointing 1957 season, Halas returned to
coach the Bears—leading them to second-place finishes in
both 1958 and 1959. In fifth place in 1960, the 1961 Bears
managed a third-place tie and tight end Mike Ditka was
voted Rookie of the Year. The following season the Bears
again held on to third place.

By the 1960s professional football was fast challenging
baseball as the national pastime. A *Newsweek* poll indicated
a wide preference for football among young adults. According to historian Charles C. Alexander, "This rising popular-

ity was a direct consequence of television's discovery of that sport. . . . Americans who'd previously seen only high-school and college football were captivated by the power and finesse of the pro game they watched on their home TV sets."

To Jack, of all the sports he broadcast, football was the most difficult. In a feature titled "The Man Who Comes to Dinner—Now and Then," he explained to the *Tribune*'s Richard Blakesley the broadcasting problems inherent in football: "The game lasts about 2½ hours, but there's only about 15 minutes of actual play. It's our job to ad-lib in the dead spots between plays and endless substitutions. And since deception is the key to the entire game, trying to keep up with the maneuverings of 22 men on the field from a press box a quarter of a mile away is tough—especially in bad weather."

In an interview with Paul Molloy of the *Sun-Times*, Jack pulled a set of numbers from his pocket and described a technique he used in broadcasting the games:

> These are the numbers of the Green Bay Packers, their positions. I carry these and the numbers of the other teams—depending who we're about to play—wherever I go. I lay them out on the desk and study them between phone calls. You're an eighth of a mile away from the play and the most important thing is identification of the players, and as far as I'm concerned they all look alike when they're that far away.

In 1963 coach Halas—often criticized, Jack remembers, for being "too old and senile to coach effectively in the NFL"—guided the Bears to a winning record from their opening victory. When the Green Bay Packers met the Bears at Wrigley Field that year, the teams were tied for first place in the Western Conference. The game was a sellout, at a time when televised games were blacked out in the home-team market. Bears fans could only listen to the Brickhouse/ Kupcinet radio broadcast—except for the four hundred enthusiasts who traveled 180 miles in chartered railroad cars and watched the game at a Galesburg, Illinois, hotel.

In the Bears' final regular-season game of 1963, a last-minute Dave Whitsell interception of the Detroit Lions won the conference title. Then, at frigid Wrigley Field, with Brickhouse and Chris Schenkel broadcasting on NBC-TV, the Bears defeated the New York Giants for the NFL championship, 14–10. It was the first Bears championship in seventeen years, and, to Jack, "Halas was where he belonged, at center stage. And because of George Allen's brilliant work as defensive coach, the players voted him the game ball."

The 1964 team stumbled to a 5–9 season but reversed the path in 1965. Jack's "biggest moment" with the Bears came against San Francisco in December of that year. In a game that ranks among the best in professional football, Bears rookie Gale Sayers became only the third player ever to run for six touchdowns. Halas was jubilant: "It was the greatest performance ever by one man on a football field; I never saw such a thing in my life!"

Another losing season in 1966 was followed by second place in 1967 and the final retirement of coach Halas. Brickhouse remembers the agony of seeing Sayers's knee collapse under a San Francisco tackle in 1968: "What might have happened if this man, whose career was terribly brief, had stayed well and had run for maybe nine years, as Jim Brown did." The Bears finished with a 7–7 record.

The worst season in the Brickhouse/Kupcinet era was in 1969. Sayers recovered sufficiently to play again, but the team won only one game while losing thirteen. To Jack, however, "that season produced one of my favorite Sayers stories. Because of the injury and operation, he was no longer the greatest open-field runner of all time—but he was determined to get his thousand yards that year. He did it, even though all of his runs were inside end or tackle or guard; he was never in the open field for any amount of time. The longest run he made from scrimmage the entire year was twenty-eight yards. Yet with his fierce determination—and even with a 1–13 ball club—Sayers got his thousand yards."

When the American Football League and National Football League merged in 1970, the Bears were placed in the Central Division of the National Conference. The team improved significantly, finishing third in its final year at Wrigley Field. Moving to Soldier Field in 1971, the Bears compiled losing records through 1975. In 1973, on the twentieth anniversary of the Brickhouse/Kupcinet team, Jack reports that "Dan Shannon, head of the Chicago Park District, put two bear cubs in the Lincoln Park Zoo and the names Kup and Brick on the plaque outside the cage. It gave Kup a line that he used on me all winter: 'The word's around now that Kup is pregnant, which gives you an idea what Brickhouse has been doing to me in that booth for twenty years.' "

The final season for Brickhouse and Kupcinet as the Bears' radio broadcasters was in 1976. The team finished 7–7, taking second place in the division. Early the next year, because the Bears' general manager wanted the games "broadcast on a station that covers no other professional sports teams," the owners transferred their longtime WGN affiliation to WBBM.

Jack received the news while vacationing in France. He told the *Sun-Times*' Bob Blanchard, "I knew the negotiations were being held, of course. But I kind of felt the Bears would hang on to wgn after all these years. . . . I feel the Bears owed it to us after 24 years to let us meet the highest offer."

A decade later, after the Bears crushed the New England Patriots 46–10 in the 1986 Super Bowl, Jack "couldn't help but hark back to 1963, when the Bears beat the New York Giants for the nfl title in the pre–Super Bowl days. He noted in *Thanks for Listening!*, "I got the feeling that somewhere up there George Halas was smiling" when his grandson, Bears' president Michael McCaskey, accepted the Super Bowl trophy. "Mike Ditka was one of my favorites as a hardnosed Bears' tight end," when Jack was broadcasting the Bears, "so it was particularly pleasing to me to watch him coach what was quite possibly the best football team ever."

Summing up their Bears assignments, Jack stated, "Kup said one time that we were there for two division titles and the 1963 championship: 'You name it, we were there—a 1–13 season, too. The whole gamut.'"

In 1946 Brickhouse was given the opportunity to broadcast basketball—his first love in sports. Maurice White, owner of the American Gear Company, also owned the Chicago American Gears of the National Basketball League. The star of the team was DePaul graduate and future Hall of Famer George Mikan. The Gears' general manager, C. Guy Grimm, described by Jack as "a Missouri horse farmer," offered him $200 per game to broadcast twenty-two games after contracting with Chicago radio station wcfl. "I thought that would be fine; it was a 50,000-watt station," Jack said. "Then Grimm told me, 'Unfortunately, we can get only an hour for each game.' I said, 'Final hour? That's all right; we'll pick it

up in the second half and give a little recap of the early scoring.' When he responded, 'We have only the first hour,' I said,
'You've got to be crazy!'"

From the International Amphitheater, Jack did, however,
broadcast the first hour of the first Gears game. "After I
signed off, the listeners were so damned incensed, I thought
they'd torch the place. Naturally the broadcast schedule was
canceled. And I had been after Grimm for a contract for
weeks, but he never came through. After that first game, I
told him, 'I'll take my pay and be on my way,' but he said,
'If you don't do the games, we can't pay you.' Both Mikan
and I pursued lawsuits against the team, but the night before
the court date White settled with us."

Fifteen years later Jack had a second offer to broadcast
professional basketball when insurance executive Dave Trager
was awarded a Chicago franchise in the National Basketball
Association. In charge of contracts for WGN, Jack "made a
deal with Trager to do ten to twelve games at a real low
price." The new Chicago Packers played the 1961–62 opening season at the amphitheater, with rookie center Walt Bel-
lamy averaging 31 points per game. "Yet," says Jack, "the
club just didn't get the press coverage it needed; plus, the NBA
wasn't all that great in those years."

For the second season and with a new name, the Zephyrs
played at the Chicago Coliseum. And with Brickhouse again
broadcasting, the team had another dismally small following. Trager and his investors "took a heck of a bath" and in
1963 sold the team—which became the Baltimore, and later
the Washington, Bullets.

In 1966 former Chicago Gears guard Dick O. Klein gam-
bled a successful business and his suburban Kenilworth home
on a new NBA team, which he named the Chicago Bulls. His

first players included Jerry Sloan, Nate Bowman, Don Kojis, Barry Clemens, Al Bianchi, Guy Rodgers, Erwin Mueller, Jim King, Bob Boozer, Jim Washington, Keith Erickson, and McCoy McLemore, and later Bobby Weiss and the great Bob Love. The first coach was John Kerr and the first television broadcaster Jack Brickhouse. He recalls,

> The Chicago Bulls became the broadcasting property of WGN in a most unusual manner. Dick Klein and I went to dinner one night at Matty's Wayside Inn on the North Shore, near where we both lived. We were going to discuss the possibility of a radio and television contract between the Bulls and WGN. Somehow we got into a little discussion about good stingers. We both liked stingers, but we had a little difference of opinion about what makes a good one. So Dick would have the bartender make one his way, I'd have him make one my way, then his way, and my way.
>
> The next thing you know, after we both had a few stingers we started to talk business. We turned over a place mat menu, and on the blank side we drew up a six-year contract for the Bulls' games to be broadcast on WGN radio and television.
>
> In our newsroom I made a Polaroid picture of the place mat, and I took the picture into a sales meeting the next morning. Our sales manager, John McDaniels, looked at me and said: "You want me to send my men out on the street to sell this feature on this basis? You're crazy!"
>
> That contract held up for six years, despite the fact that Klein's co-owners were not happy about it, because he had a better money offer from another

station. But Dick realized that WGN was better for the exposure the Bulls needed at that early time in their development.

The Bulls and WGN announced a thirty-game television package, plus radio coverage of all home and selected road games. From St. Louis, Jack telecast the first Bulls game, played against the Hawks in October 1966, and he was jubilant in announcing the 104–97 victory. Back in Chicago, only 350 season tickets were sold prior to the home opener at the amphitheater. The Bulls won the game and went on to a winning first season and the NBA playoffs. John Kerr was named coach of the year.

For their second season the Bulls moved to Chicago Stadium. After a losing start the team recovered to make the playoffs again; Kerr again won the coaching award. But throughout the early years, Jack said, "attendance was a big problem. Our gates were anywhere from four to eight or nine thousand." Some games drew fewer than a thousand fans.

Following the second season Kerr resigned and was replaced by college basketball coach Dick Motta. The *Chicago Tribune*'s Bob Logan was the only reporter who traveled with the team. In *The Bulls and Chicago: A Stormy Affair*, Logan wrote that at the time Motta took over,

> the Bulls were a million light years from being mentioned in the same sentence with the established entries. They just didn't count, and few believed they'd survive long enough to do so. . . .
> Public confidence in the Bulls' stability had sunk so low that Klein couldn't find new backers

to buy out his partners. Instead, [in 1969] they decided to get rid of him. From that moment on, Motta was the main man in the franchise, pushing the team steadily toward respectability and eventual acceptance. . . .

Jack Brickhouse aired the games and peddled the Bulls with the same gusto that marked long years of sunny-side-up delivery for the Cubs and Bears. If ever a team needed that sort of buildup, especially in the formative years, it was the Bulls. Hard-core cage fans expressing annoyance at Brickhouse's unfamiliarity with pro rules were far outnumbered by those who liked his positive approach.

Jack, who was assisted on radio by Lou Boudreau, relishes his early association with the team. In his foreword to Logan's book, Jack wrote:

The Bulls and their predecessors had to start from scratch, behind the biggest eight ball of them all. There was no way pro basketball was going to make the grade in Chicago. Way back when Bruce Hale, Rick Barry's father-in-law, played on the same American Gears team with George Mikan and Dick Klein, they faded out. The Chicago Stags . . . couldn't survive. Even before that, George Halas's Chicago pro basketball efforts failed. The only money to be made playing basketball in Chicago was the under-the-table buck earned by amateurs using phony names. . . .

They forgot to tell one man that it couldn't be done . . . a zealot named Dick Klein . . . with a wide-eyed school-boy trust in his fellowman and his own passion for an upfront sports spotlight.

Among Jack's recollections:

I remember at Madison Square Garden one night a
game between the Bulls and the New York Knicks.
Instead of a courtside setup, they had us way up in
the back of the place, high in the second level. There
were some twenty-five seats in front of us where if
anybody stood up they would block our view. I got
there early, took a look at it, and said, "For God's
sake, sell me those seats; we can't have that happening." They finally adjusted the seats and blocked them
off for us.

One of the highlight moments was when the Bulls
went to the West Coast and were playing the Los
Angeles Lakers and were on the verge of making the
championship series. For my color man I hired the
great basketball player Elgin Baylor (now, by the way,
general manager of the Los Angeles Clippers). He
came through beautifully. The Bulls had an 8-point
lead with about four minutes to play, when Elgin
said, "The Bulls are standing around on defense. If
they don't start moving better, they are going to lose
the game." Well, they didn't start moving. They were
still standing around, by Elgin's standards, and sure
enough, they lost that game.

One of our scariest moments was in Philadelphia.
They had just opened their new stadium, the Spec-
trum. All of a sudden during the game a huge sheet
of steel fell from the ceiling, landing on the court.
Thank God, nobody was touched by it.

I had some great times, some real fun moments,
with the Bulls. We knew that someday they would be

an important feature in Chicago, and sure enough, they're a sellout every time. I even had one or two sellouts before my contract was up.

In the summer of 1972 the team was purchased by a group that included Chicago Blackhawks owner Arthur Wirtz. Instead of renewing with WGN, the investors contracted with Channel 44 and WIND radio, which agreed to carry the entire team schedule.

In 1979 the authors of *Who Runs Chicago?* wrote: "The Chicago Bulls are widely considered the worst team in professional basketball, but Bull fans remain bullish. Chicago fans learn to savor victory as a rare vintage; as sportswriter Don Pierson holds: 'In Chicago, any victory, any way, any time, any place, any sport, is a big deal.' " Today the Chicago Bulls—with consecutive sellout games since 1987—have won more championships in fewer than thirty years than any other professional sports team in the city's history.

CHAPTER 8

Politics and
Personalities

FROM THE START OF HIS CAREER BRICKHOUSE DID NOT limit his broadcasting to one specialty—even though he became known primarily as a sports announcer. He made deliberate and ongoing commitments to public affairs as well as commercial assignments, on both radio and television. Even in the Peoria days he had broadcast interviews with local businesspeople and live remotes of area events. His coverage of the 1944 national nominating conventions in Chicago brought recognition for political reporting. Acquaintanceships and friendships with governors, mayors, clergy, business leaders, and celebrities led to lucrative assignments in the increasingly competitive broadcast field.

In the early 1950s well-known Chicago radio personality Ernie Simon moved to WGN from WJJD, where he and Bob Elson had partnered on the Elson-Simon variety show. As a teenager Simon had been a vaudeville performer and then was teamed with and tutored by one of the original "Three Stooges." Turned down for military service during World War II because of poor eyesight, he became a war hero on

the North Africa staff of British Field Marshal Bernard
Montgomery. At WGN, Simon and Brickhouse cohosted the
afternoon "Brickhouse-Simon Show," and to Jack, "Simon
was a talented disk jockey and comedian." His wife, Patricia Simon Newman, recalls that "Ernest was a great talent,
the quickest mind I've ever known. In those pioneer days of
television, he and Jack walked right in. They all worked
themselves to the bone trying to make inroads—Dave Gar-
roway, Mike Wallace. I thought they were successful at that
time; I had no idea what they would become."

Radio listeners found the "Brickhouse-Simon Show"
hilarious, according to Newman. "People told me they pulled
off on the shoulder of Lake Shore Drive because they were
laughing so hard. There was a chemistry between Ernest and
Jack, and Ernest was completely in love with what they did."

Two years later Simon accepted an offer at WBKB-TV, and
Jack found a new radio partner in WGN's morning disk jockey,
Eddie Hubbard. The two combined for several years on the
"Brickhouse-Hubbard Show," with banter, news, and popu-
lar music (but, by executive order, "no rock and roll"). Jack
remains in awe of his former partner's knowledge of music.
Today Hubbard is a well-known disk jockey throughout the
South, syndicated from a Dallas, Texas, radio station.

In 1956 WGN left the Mutual network to once again oper-
ate as an independent station. Frank Schreiber was succeeded
as vice president and general manager by Ward Quaal, who
in 1941 had begun his radio career with WGN and returned
after four years as vice president of WLW in Cincinnati. In
expanding the WGN staff, he announced the hiring of two former WLW colleagues, Wally Phillips and Bob Bell. Jack
remembers the reaction:

We at the station received this news with a certain amount of skepticism: the fact that they were successful in Cincinnati didn't mean they were good enough to work Chicago. Wally Phillips, as it turned out, became the greatest single radio talent the city of Chicago has ever known. And Bob Bell was unbelievably talented as "Bozo the Clown," as host of "The Three Stooges," and on other programs as a sidekick, a personality, a comedian. It's impossible to overemphasize the talent value that these two men represented not only to WGN radio and television but also to the broadcasting industry in this city.

During the late 1950s Jack worked assignments with both Phillips and Bell and once again hosted "Man on the Street," demonstrating his easy audience rapport. Then in the summer of 1960 he covered the Democratic national convention in Los Angeles. Among the several presidential candidates were Hubert Humphrey, Lyndon Johnson, Stuart Symington, John F. Kennedy, and, for a time, the 1952 and 1956 nominee, Adlai E. Stevenson.

Former president Harry S Truman, "just trying to put a little fight" into the proceedings, charged that the convention was rigged for Kennedy by his influential father, Joseph P. Kennedy. Interviewing former Roosevelt campaign manager James Farley, Jack asked his reaction to the charge. Jack recalled Farley's cordial response, "Well, now, as one who has rigged one or two myself, what's wrong with it?"

After a raucous demonstration by Stevenson partisans, reminiscent to Brickhouse of the demonstration he had witnessed for favorite son Scott Lucas in 1944, Kennedy won the nomination on the first ballot. The broadcaster's WGN convention coverage was termed by one media reviewer "the best in the country."

In the November election Kennedy was victorious, as was the Illinois Democratic gubernatorial candidate, Otto Kerner. Kerner and Brickhouse had developed a casual friendship several years earlier when both were members of a Chicago-area country club. Kerner was a "very well-liked man," Jack recalls, "with the good looks of a John Wayne or a Gary Cooper; he might have been a great presidential prospect. We all realized back then that someday television would have a role in electing presidents."

As a boxing fan as well as a fight announcer, Jack did not agree with the many citizens who wanted to ban the sport in Illinois. He telephoned the newly elected Kerner:

> "Governor, for what it's worth, I recommend that you not outlaw boxing. If you do, we will again have what we had once before—illegal, bootleg boxing in barnyards and on barges. I suggest that you have a commission make some rules changes regarding medical attention for the fighters." About three weeks later Kerner called: "Whenever you're ready, I'll name you chairman of the state boxing commission." I answered, "Governor, I wasn't looking for a job. I'm going to have to first check it out here at the station."
>
> The WGN officials at Tribune Tower thought that it could be a conflict to have as a commissioner someone who makes part of his living covering sports, including boxing. I wasn't surprised, and I understood.

In August 1964, after a White Sox doubleheader, Jack traveled to Atlantic City, New Jersey, to cover another Democratic national convention. This time he reported on Lyndon Johnson's nomination as the peace candidate, during the American troop buildup in southeast Asia.

Between convention proceedings, Jack lined up an interview with Governor Kerner, who was running for a second term. "I remember broadcasting the interview from those chairs on the boardwalk. It was a good interview; he was a solid guy." That November, Kerner won reelection, only the second Democratic governor reelected in Illinois in more than one hundred years.

Several weeks after the Democratic convention Jack crossed the country for the Republican national convention in San Francisco and the nomination of conservative Barry Goldwater. Interviewing vice presidential nominee William E. Miller, Jack heard one of his favorite quotations: "I'm a Roman Catholic, and Barry Goldwater is Episcopalian and Jewish. Anyone who votes against this ticket is a bigot."

Jack's most memorable convention interview, however, was one he and WGN's Washington bureau chief Bob Foster recorded with former president Dwight D. Eisenhower. After discussing his role in the upcoming campaign, he was asked by Jack about "the relationship and the value of sports in the world today." Eisenhower's taped response was based on his own experience.

> Well, first of all, you know that as President I started a committee for youth fitness. . . . Instead of having children enjoying their sports vicariously by sitting in the stands and watching some students—to get more intramural, more genuine participation on a widespread basis. I believe that as

you get a little older, leadership qualities are developed very well in sports. [Team sports] are really splendid for delivering or developing those traits of character that make it possible for you to work with your halfback, or with the fullback, and the rest of them. And I think they're not only good for physical development, but they're good for quickening the mind and making it alert to emergency situations.

After the official interview, Jack commented to Eisenhower:

> "Mr. President, I understand, if you read the box score of a certain Kansas professional baseball team, you'll see a fellow in right field with the very unimaginative alias of D. Brown, and D. Brown was really D. Eisenhower, picking up a buck on the side in the summer." Somewhat surprised at my knowledge of the story, Eisenhower admitted to it. "There were three of us; it was common practice in those days. It lasted about three or four weeks. We got to play a little baseball in the summer, pick up a few dollars. But we had to change our names, of course, in order to maintain our college eligibility."

In the mid-1960s, while broadcasting for both the Sox and the Cubs, Jack also served two terms as president of the Chicago chapter of the National Academy of Television Arts and Sciences. Those combined duties produced an amusing series of encounters with a United States senator:

> Paul Douglas of Illinois was a great baseball fan. One day while working at Sox Park, I spotted him in one of the low boxes and sent my runner to invite

him up. When he came to the booth, we let him broadcast a Sox half inning. Don Buford hit a home run—so we gave the senator credit for Buford's good luck.

Two weeks later at Wrigley Field, I looked down at the low boxes, and there was Senator Douglas. I sent him a note: "The Cubs demand equal time." He came up and did a half inning again—and Ernie Banks hit a home run.

That winter for the annual Chicago Emmy Awards we created a new category, "Most Promising Rookie Baseball Announcer," and gave the award to Douglas. He showed up to accept it! He was a heck of a guy.

Along with sports schedules, Jack hosted "Jack Brickhouse Reports," a nightly program of more than three hundred interviews from locations in Chicago and around the world. His guests ranged from the archbishop of Canterbury to Jack Dempsey, Gerald Ford to Gloria Swanson, Joe Louis to Jerry Lewis.

His proudest achievement on "Jack Brickhouse Reports" came in 1965, a Vatican audience with Pope Paul VI. Jack's attendance at the audience and permission to record it had been prearranged through Joseph Meegan of the Chicago Back of the Yards Neighborhood Council and his friend Monsignor Paul Marcinkus of the papal staff. Seated with Nelda "at the foot of the throne" after taping other Vatican ceremonies, Jack recorded the papal message. "It was fantastic." He carried the tape back to Chicago and had it delivered to the archdiocesan office, where students of Father John Banahan translated the Latin message into English. Broadcast on WGN on Palm Sunday and then produced as a record album, the program won an international broadcasting award.

During their European trip the Brickhouses were in London when Prime Minister Winston Churchill died. Jack gave a live WGN report on the funeral ceremonies, as well as segments from the House of Commons and Office of the Lord Mayor and interviews with Britons standing outside the Parliament building and Buckingham Palace.

Another Brickhouse series in 1965 was the "Man on the Street" interviews he conducted in twelve countries. Carrying portable recording equipment and assisted by interpreters, Jack asked about perceptions of the United States. "I met quite a few people in other parts of the world who didn't know the name of our president," a surprising revelation to the man who had become acquainted with several presidents through his coverage of political conventions.

In early 1967, in Paris for "Jack Brickhouse Reports," he interviewed actor Richard Burton during filming of the movie *The Comedians.* Jack introduced his program by stating, "Whenever I run into someone like him, I want to talk about acting. I run into Richard Burton, he wants to talk about baseball. I had no idea that a man from Wales, and who's spent all the time you have in England, would have interest other than in, we'll say, rugby or soccer or golf or something like that in sports. Richard?"

Burton responded with a surprising commentary:

> Well, a curious thing happened about fifteen years ago. I was doing a play on Broadway called *The Leaves Are Not for Burning.* I left it early; I left it after about three months, and everybody gave me presents, as they always do. The stage manager gave me an encyclopedia of baseball, which I'd never seen—I mean the game I'd never seen.

And I'm a voracious reader—*omnivorous*, I think, is a better word. I'll read anything; I'm an expert on the back of sauce bottles and things like that.

And I ran out of reading matter about a year later. I lived in Switzerland at the time, and I suddenly saw this book, which I hadn't read. I began to read it; read the laws of the game and so on. I thought, Well, let me see if I can figure it out. I got a drawing board and a large piece of paper and drew the diamond and began to play imaginary games. Then I couldn't wait for my next engagement in New York in order to see a real live game. Indeed, I was very lucky. The first game I saw was the first World Series that the Dodgers won against the Yankees. And since I was on Broadway at the time, I was able to see the games both at Ebbets Field and at the Yankee Stadium. And, of course, as you know, it went the whole seven games. Everything happened in it, from, I believe, Jack Robinson stealing home. I'm not absolutely sure of my details now, but anyway I fell madly in love with the game and still am in love with it.

Jack then said, "I got a kick out of your story about interesting Elizabeth Taylor in baseball. Can you tell us that one?" Burton again:

Ah, yes. She's a real philistine for an American, because she'd never seen a game. I was doing *Hamlet* in New York about two years ago, and every Sunday afternoon, of course, was devoted to watching either the Mets or the Yankees play baseball. And she became a little fed up with the whole thing and said, "Sunday afternoons are such a bloody great crashing bore now that you watch those damn games." So, I said, "Well, if you want to be a really good wife, you know, you should learn to develop my interests, so why don't you watch the game, and I'll teach you about it." So we watched the first game, and she was sort of vaguely interested. It was a doubleheader. It was the Mets against Pittsburgh, I think.

And the second game came up, and it got to the ninth inning, bottom of the ninth, and she said, "When is it going to be over?" There was no score, or maybe it was 1–1, I'm not sure. I said, "Well, it's sudden death now; any minute now it'll be over." Then it went tenth, eleventh, fifteenth, nineteenth. I think it actually went to twenty-four innings. And though it's not the world's record for the number of innings, I believe it's the world's record for the longest game ever played. I remember that game, and that was the last time she ever wanted to see baseball.

I did persuade her to go and see the Dodgers in Los Angeles. She wanted to see a fellow that she had seen on television with me that she still calls "Sneaky." "Sneaky" is Maury Wills [at that time the game's champion base stealer].

For several years beginning in the late 1960s, Jack hosted "Your F.B.I.," weekly WGN radio interviews about operations of the bureau. His guest on the Sunday evening programs was the Chicago special agent in charge, often accompanied by another special agent. The interview subjects ranged from bank robberies to child molestations, with the agents discussing ways to prevent crimes and assist law enforcement officers. Jack "got to know the agents and wound up with a fantastic admiration and respect for them."

Two of the agents once asked to use the Comiskey Park broadcast booth for surveillance of a fugitive they suspected would be at a Yankee-Sox doubleheader. Jack recalls that with their binoculars the agents "spotted him in the second inning of game one, but they didn't nail him until late in the second game!"

Agents assigned to the FBI's organized crime team were frequent guests on the program. After retirement William Roemer relived his Chicago career as a bestselling author of crime stories. A Roemer partner, John Bassett, recalled the WGN show: "Jack did a real professional job of running the FBI radio program. He knew the right questions, knew how to draw out the story so it was interesting. We taped several programs at once, and we could listen to them a couple of days later. It was a unique program, especially during that time of J. Edgar Hoover."

Bassett knew of no similar broadcasts in other cities, and that Hoover even allowed the public discussion of bureau operations is surprising.

In 1968 Jack was assigned by WGN to the national conventions of both parties. In Miami Beach, "everyone knew Richard Nixon would be the candidate." Jack wanted to interview him and asked for help from W. Clement Stone, a Chicago friend and major Republican fund-raiser. Stone, according to Jack, angered reporters and Nixon staffers by arranging an exclusive interview after the nomination.

During the balloting Nixon was secluded in his hotel suite, while Jack and the WGN audio and camera crews prepared for the interview. After securing the nomination, Nixon walked down a flight of stairs to the WGN suite, then spoke with Jack about the upcoming campaign for several minutes before moving on to announce Spiro Agnew as his running mate. Jack immediately sent the film and audiotape to WGN for radio and television broadcasts.

Compared with what was to occur at the Democratic convention that summer, the Republicans had conducted an insulated affair. The Miami convention center was protected from picketers and potential rioters by a newly constructed six-foot-high chain-link fence. Security was tight, and only credentialed persons were admitted.

In Chicago, security was also a priority. Because of intense opposition to the Vietnam War, President Lyndon Johnson had decided not to run for reelection. His vice president, Hubert Humphrey, became the nominee amid protests and clashes between the Chicago police and activist demonstrators. Jack recalls:

I was covering baseball, but because the convention was in Chicago I didn't have to take time off; I did them both. That was when the group of seven— Abbie Hoffman, Jerry Rubin, people like that—organized terrible demonstrations.

We knew the convention was going to be rough, because the FBI kept tabs on those people. I was at dinner at Ward Quaal's house (he was president of WGN); one of the guests was Marlin Johnson, head of the Chicago FBI. Johnson was called to the phone several times during the evening because one of the known agitators heading for Chicago had been seen in a hardware store in Oklahoma and then leaving with what appeared to be containers of bad-smelling liquid. That was why Mayor Daley arranged to have the National Guard hold their encampment exercises not far from the Chicago Amphitheater.

A fine young cop penetrated the Hoffman and

Rubin group; he got to be one of them and learned their secrets. He reported that one of the network producers from New York told them to start their demonstration at the Hilton Hotel around 4:30 in the afternoon at the southwest corner, because the light from the sun "will be to our benefit, and we'll give you the coverage."

When I learned about it, I made a speech during a Cubs-Houston game, saying that I was ashamed of my own profession—of the tricks of some super-liberal network people.

Many viewers didn't think my comments were appropriate for a baseball game. The WGN switchboard lit up, and I became embroiled in something of an issue. But my ballpark speech was read into the *Congressional Record* by Congressman John Kluczynski.

In 1976 Jerry Rubin, a defendant in the 1971 "Chicago Seven" trial, wrote a *Chicago Sun-Times* guest column in which he made an admission about the convention.

> All during the Chicago conspiracy trial, I was secretly rooting for the prosecution. Not because I loved the government so much, but because the prosecution was right all along. The prosecutors said we came to Chicago with the express purpose of disrupting the city, all planned out in advance. That is absolutely correct. . . .
>
> "Guilty," though, does not mean "wrong." Chicago's officials and Chicago's police reacted just as we knew they would—in a manner that exposed all the darker sides of our country. . . . I

think Chicago 1968 was an important development in helping the United States into a period of
change and self-examination.

Following the summer disruption in Chicago, in January
1969 Jack received the pleasant assignment of emceeing a
Nixon inaugural ball in Washington, D.C. At the Mayflower
Hotel in white tie and tails, he helped entertain massive
crowds of ballgoers from nine states. The *Tribune* reported
that Republican Illinois governor Richard J. Ogilvie "was a
magnet for the Illinois guests" and Senator Everett Dirksen,
"booming mightily, led some singing."

In 1972 former Illinois governor Kerner, then a federal
judge, was indicted on bribery, mail fraud, and tax evasion
charges relating to his gubernatorial term. He asked Jack
to testify on his behalf. "I answered, 'Absolutely, yes.' Your
friends are your friends, and the man was a good man. That
raised a few eyebrows around wGN, for one of their vice
presidents and so-called talents to be involved in something
like that, but as it turned out they kind of respected me
for it."

On February 9, 1973, the twenty-seventh day of the trial,
following character witnesses that included General William
Westmoreland, federal judges, college presidents, a minister,
and the executive director of the National Association for the
Advancement of Colored People, Jack was called to the stand.
According to the *Sun-Times'* Tom Fitzpatrick, "The effect on
the jury was electric. As one, they sat erect in their chairs,
recognizing Brickhouse at once. There has been a parade of
prominent people as character witnesses in the trial, but
none of them was so immediately recognizable to the jury."
Jack testified that he had known Kerner for approximately

twenty-five years, "principally as a friend," and in answer to the defense attorney's query said that Kerner's reputation for honesty and integrity was "absolutely the highest."

The prosecutor, United States Attorney James R. Thompson—who went on to become the longest-serving governor in Illinois history—began his brief cross-examination by stating, "I'd feel foolish calling you anything but Jack." Fitzpatrick concluded his report on the day's testimony: "If the surface reaction of the jurors means anything, Brickhouse may have done more for Judge Kerner's fortunes in two minutes than he has been able to do for the Cubs' pennant chances in 20 years."

Jack's recollection of the trial is tinged with sadness over the verdict:

> I remember a couple of things about the trial. Number one, only one person on that jury had as much as a year of college, yet they had volumes of testimony to try to digest. And number two—there are times when something like this makes sense and other times when it might not—instead of hiring a local lawyer, Kerner went with the Edward Bennett Williams firm in Washington, D.C. Wouldn't it have been better for him to have used a popular local lawyer, my thinking being that some people may get the idea that if you go to Washington, calling in all those heavyweights, maybe you're a little afraid that you have done something wrong?
>
> Anyway, the poor guy didn't have a chance. There were numerous counts against him. The way the charges were packaged, he was either guilty or not

guilty of all of them. That is, I suppose, what made
it difficult for the public to understand.

In November 1973 Daisy Brickhouse died of a stroke at
her Chicago apartment. She had moved from Peoria years
earlier and worked until retirement at the Ambassador East
Hotel. Daisy and Jack remained close throughout her life,
and on many weekends she visited him, Nelda, and Jeanne
at their Wilmette home—reminiscing about Peoria and
Daisy's brief marriage to the salesman Will Brickhouse: "I
wish I had him now; I'd handle him." Her sudden death was
a difficult loss for Jack. He dedicated his autobiography
Thanks for Listening! to Daisy: "God couldn't be everywhere, so He created Mothers."

Five years later, in 1978, Jack and Nelda Brickhouse ended
their lengthy marriage. One regret about his career was the
time it took from his family, "but your job is your job." Their
daughter Jeanne graduated from Augustana College and
added masters' degrees from the University of Missouri, then
became a schoolteacher and counselor. She is married to
Alfredo Jimenez, a concert musician. Her son from her previous marriage, Noah Schuffman, is a teenager with scholas-
tic and athletic abilities—and is the pride of his grandfather.

Brickhouse met Patricia Ettelson when he substituted for
their mutual friend Irv Kupcinet at a special appearance she
had arranged. A publicist and Northwestern University graduate, Pat was reared in Omaha, Nebraska, the only child of
Sylvia and Leslie Lawrence Burkenroad. Leslie had been an
All-American basketball player at the University of Nebraska.
Pat Ettelson has three children and five grandchildren. In
1980 she and Jack were married in Palm Springs, California.

The approximately fifty guests, including many Chicagoans, were all invited to serve as maids of honor and best men.

Jack calls Pat his "close friend, in a marriage that really works. And she has a big interest in sports." Pat reciprocates the affection: "After fifteen years, we're still on cloud nine."

In 1981 Brickhouse renewed his acquaintance with a fellow 1930s broadcaster, President Ronald Reagan. During his five-year career at WHO in Des Moines, Iowa, Reagan announced more than five hundred Cubs games, re-created from wire reports. Jack enjoyed the White House reunion:

Somebody going through the files of *The Sporting News* found that exactly fifty years earlier Dutch Reagan had won a *Sporting News* broadcasting award. They decided to reproduce the award and give it to him at a White House luncheon, with some of his sports broadcasting contemporaries—Mel Allen, Red Barber, Ernie Harwell, Byron Saam, and Brickhouse.

There were also veteran sportswriters like Bob Broeg from St. Louis, Dick Young and Joe Reichler from New York, Shirley Povich from D.C., Joe McGuff from Kansas City, Allen Lewis from Philadelphia, Earl Lawson from Cincinnati, Edgar Munzel from Chicago, Cy Burick from Dayton, and several *Sporting News* officials, along with Vice President George Bush and adviser Patrick Buchanan.

President Reagan came into the room, shook hands with everyone, sat down, then set the tone: "Well, fellows, if I'd stayed in the business with you, maybe now I wouldn't be living in public housing."

That was the most serious remark of the whole luncheon. I don't think the president had laughed that much in years.

Later in 1981, the national Broadcast Pioneers organization honored Reagan, and Jack was again among the White House guests. Reagan told several nostalgic broadcasting stories and amid much laughter from his contemporaries claimed credit for describing the first instant replay—a track meet he broadcast from Drake University in Des Moines:

> All afternoon I'd been touting the quarter-mile at Drake, because we were competing with the Penn Relays; those two events always took place on the same day. They brought in the president of Drake University, and he welcomed our radio audience. (Incidentally, we were broadcasting both events. Bill Stern . . . was at Penn, I was at Drake, and we'd switch back and forth. It was on NBC.)
>
> He talked right through that quarter-mile event. I didn't have the heart to tell him, the president of Drake University. I knew it had to take about forty-eight seconds; the event was all over. I said, "There they go, they're coming around the track. . . ." I brought them in—one, two, three. But I had dead silence from the crowd, because nothing was going on, so, I explained that as "the crowd was stunned by the sheer drama of it!"

Brickhouse and Reagan have maintained contact. In 1994 videotaped congratulations from the president highlighted a dinner honoring Jack and Pat Brickhouse for their volunteer work on behalf of Illinois war veterans' organizations.

CHAPTER 9

Jack and Harry

O NE RAINY CHICAGO DAY IN AUTUMN 1993, JACK
Brickhouse and Harry Caray met for lunch and the
opportunity to reminisce about their lengthy sportscasting
careers. Brickhouse and his former crosstown compatriot
greeted each other warmly, two men from similar midwestern backgrounds. Caray, three years younger, was born in St.
Louis, the son of Daisy and Christopher Carabina. Orphaned
at the age of eight, Harry was reared by an aunt. Jack and
his young mother, Daisy, were living in Peoria at the time.

The names of both Caray and Brickhouse are synonymous with baseball, although both also broadcast other
sports. Harry's career began in his hometown in 1944, when
he was hired at WIL radio for fall and winter sports, primarily
basketball and bowling. Learning that the Griesedieck family, owners of the St. Louis Baseball Cardinals, needed an
announcer for the 1945 season, he applied directly to club
president Ed Griesedieck.

Harry got the job and was the KMOX radio voice of the
Cardinals for years. In Chicago, after WGN decided not to
carry baseball, Jack moved to WJJD in 1945 to broadcast the

White Sox. That season was thus a prime subject for reminiscing. Brickhouse to Caray: "I've been in this town following the Cubs for over half a century, and I'm still waiting to work my first Cub pennant. The one they won, I wasn't around. So you and I both had a memorable 1945 season."

Jack and Harry compared notes on the Midwest's best-known baseball broadcaster of the 1930s and 1940s, Bob Elson. To Jack, Elson was the master, "the most imitated baseball broadcaster in history, whose pleasant, melodious voice never changed in a half century behind the mike." To Harry, Elson did alter his manner of broadcasting after serving in World War II. "He wasn't the same announcer when he came back. He changed his whole style. He used to be very enthusiastic; then I think he tried to be different— absolutely different—from Bert Wilson, who was a good announcer. I think Elson tried to be so different from Wilson that it affected his work."

Jack responded: "When Wilson first came up, he sounded like a pup out of Elson. Wilson admitted that he'd listen to Bob and imitate him. Also, Bob was no kid by then. He was twelve or thirteen years older than I was, and so in 1946 I would have been thirty, he would have been in his forties. Some guys slow up, you know, a lot sooner than others, and Bob kind of slowed up after that." Harry disagreed: "I don't think he slowed up through age. I think he slowed up because he deliberately wanted to be different. . . . But he was a good one before he went into the service."

They did agree, however, on one Elson trait. Harry: "He had a great sense of humor, great laugh." Jack: "When he started to giggle, you could have lost your best friend and you'd still have to laugh with him; it was contagious."

Jack and Harry shared memories of a great event at Wrigley Field: Stan Musial's 3,000th career hit. According to

Jack, Cardinals manager Fred Hutchinson "wanted to save Musial for his 3,000th hit the next day in St. Louis. He wasn't even in the dugout; he was sitting with the pitchers in the bullpen, sunning himself." Harry continued: "They called him in the ninth inning to pinch hit. He got a double down the left field line that I think drove in the tying and winning runs." After the May 15, 1958, game, Caray joined Brickhouse on the field for a televised interview with Musial. Jack recalls that day as a highlight of his own career.

Harry also remembered the Cardinals trip to St. Louis that evening. "The train made about eight stops. Everywhere, the whole town was there to yell at Stan, congratulate him. It was like a triumphant parade. Everywhere the train stopped, people were gathered, thousands and thousands."

Harry's story prompted a related reminiscence from Jack: "You know, I learned more baseball on trains than I did anyplace else, because you'd sit with the managers, the coaches, some of the players, with the guys in the club car, the smoker, or even in the dining car. You could get up to walk around, and guys mixed. You can't do that today on airplanes."

"The game has changed," Harry continued. "Now ballplayers aren't together as much as they used to be. As a matter of fact, you've had more cliques. . . . The Dominicans couldn't speak English, they stuck together. The Spanish couldn't speak English, they stuck together. And now it's money and changing teams. Seeing a Stan Musial with one team, a Ted Williams with one team, you'll never see that again."

Harry went on, "It's unconscionable that ballplayers haven't got the time to sign a little kid's autograph. Do you know why they don't do it now? Their agents advise them not to, because it lessens their worth when they go to those card shows. Now you're getting down to ownership and management, which is all bottom-line. You know, the old-time owner may not have been as rich as they are today, but he was more of a sportsman. You know, like Wrigley, Calvin Griffith, Tom Yawkey, or even Gussie Busch in his own way."

Jack responded: "But sometimes maybe we criticize the corporate guys a little bit more than they should be criticized. Here's what I mean. OK, the corporation buys the ball club; but the guy who is CEO or the guy who is vice president in charge of that ball club corporation is really one heck of a baseball fan. He's a guy with a little background, maybe played in school, or is just a nutty fan. He's got to be a bottom-line guy, we know that, but he's not totally cold-blooded."

Harry asked: "Do you remember, when the *Tribune* bought the Cubs, the ridiculous story that they were going to build a barrier to keep the people on the rooftops from seeing the ball game? What the hell kind of thinking was that? That's one of the mystiques of Wrigley Field. You look out and you see them on the rooftops, drinking, eating some barbecue, having fun. The total involved is less than five hundred people. Here's a ballpark full with thirty-two thousand, thirty-five thousand; now—especially for those who are in the people business—that's ridiculous, but that's corporate thinking. . . . I went to Jim Frey and raised holy hell. I said, 'You guys have to be nuts.' I asked, 'What's wrong with it? No other team in the history of baseball has had this.' Then, suddenly, that idea died a quiet death. And, you know, I think general managers as a rule really know their business, but if they are handicapped by the owners—you can't spend this, you can't spend that—you're not going to have success."

The conversation evolved into a discussion of ball game attendance. Harry: "Look at the problem of the Cubs, Jack.

They just finished the [1993] season. They drew 2,700,000; they averaged 34,000 per day played. If they draw capacity for the eighty-one games, they'll draw another 200,000 people. So, the difference between winning and losing up until now hasn't been important at the gate. But if they keep losing and those guys on the south side keep winning, eventually the Cubs are going to go down the drain. They'd better realize it."

Jack: "It happened once before. There was a time, you know, when the Cubs could automatically draw a million. But all of a sudden 750,000, 780,000 for a couple of years. They were down." Harry remembered the weekends when Lou Breese and his orchestra entertained at Cubs games. "It would be a gorgeous day at Wrigley Field. Announcing for the Cardinals, I would say, 'Gee, just to hear the music and sit in the sunshine, you'd think there'd be more people than this.' They'd have 2,500 on a Friday; that's the year they drew 500,000 people."

Jack: "I was at a party one time with Helen Wrigley—who was a fan, by the way—Phil's wife. She asked, 'Why aren't we drawing more people?' And I answered, 'Well, Helen, when I sit in that booth and I look out at the bleachers, I don't see enough hand-holding.' She said, 'What do you mean?' I said, 'Up until the last year or two, it's been very fashionable for a young guy to take his girlfriend to the ballpark and sit in those bleachers at Wrigley Field; young kids, the teenagers, and the young college kids. I'm not seeing them out there anymore; they've found other places to go. You'd better hope that they'll come back.' Well, eventually they did come back. As a matter of fact, Phil Wrigley himself really liked those kids. He filled a charter plane one time and flew them all to Atlanta, the 'bleacher bums,' for a series down there, that kind of stuff."

Harry: "I met him, but I really didn't know him. I've often wondered whether he was a great visionary or whether he was just lucky. Either way, you have to give him all the credit in the world, because what's made the Cubs has been daytime baseball. Even to this day the Giants can't draw at night at Candlestick Park. They played fifty-three day games this year, trying to turn it around. And they did draw more than they had last year."

Jack: "Look at the Boston Red Sox, Fenway Park, afternoons. A small ballpark, Thursday afternoon, Wednesday afternoon, thirty-two thousand, thirty-three thousand."

Harry: "Not only that; you're drawing the people who are your fans for a lifetime, the little kids. They get on the el in the suburbs, get off at Wrigley Field, watch a ballgame, they're home by 5:30. Can you imagine a little kid who's been to Wrigley Field? Back at home, he's got something to talk about with his parents: 'You should have seen Ryne Sandberg! You should have seen Mark Grace!' They might have nothing to talk about if it weren't for baseball."

Jack: "And you can give the kid a couple, three dollars, put him on the el, know that he's going to be home for dinner; and he's going to do it all in the daytime, when it's safe."

Harry: "Look at what we have, a World Series at night. Who the hell can keep a kid up that long? Even on weekends, at night. . . . Now we're in the Series; every game is at night. And we had an hour delay last night [October 11, 1993]. How would you like to have a kid out on a school night when you're trying to discourage that kind of hours, taking him out, keeping him out that late to see a ball game?"

Jack: "Phil Wrigley owned the Los Angeles franchise in the Pacific Coast League, had a Wrigley Field out there. He went there one time—Bob Sheffing was managing the ball-

club, John Holland was his general manager—and they filled
the ballpark, fourteen thousand or whatever. They were real
happy, with the boss there to see this big crowd. As they were
walking out after the game, John said, 'Well, I hope you
enjoyed yourself tonight, Mr. Wrigley. We're pretty proud of
that crowd.' Phil said, 'Yes, very nice, but where were the
children?' Where were the children? Not in that neighborhood, not at night. But he pinpointed something important."

Harry answered, "Day baseball really made the Cubs."
Then he returned to the subject of Phil Wrigley. "I asked you
whether he was that man of great vision or whether maybe
it was just a little luck." Jack: "Well, maybe a little of both,
Harry. He *was* a visionary guy."

Harry recalled: "I know that when he opened it up for
television coverage, he opened it up to anybody, and radio,
too." Brickhouse: "Damn right. You know, he once threatened to pull his ball club out of the National League and play
independent ball if they wouldn't let him do radio broadcasts.
The other owners argued: 'Why give your product away?' "

Harry: "I remember [Cardinals president] Sam Breadon.
He had the famous Gashouse Gang, and one year he said he
was not going to broadcast, because it would keep people
from coming to the ballpark. With the famous Gashouse
Gang, he drew three hundred thousand people, the lowest
attendance in the history of St. Louis baseball."

Jack added: "I had an experience with Breadon one time.
In those days we broadcast the ball club that was in town
on WGN radio. This one day the Sox were in town but were
rained out. The Cubs were playing in St. Louis, so we set up
the Western Union ticker at the studio for the Cubs-St. Louis
game. All of a sudden Sam Breadon, who found out we were
broadcasting the game, claimed that we overlapped into his

territory because WGN was a 50,000-watt station; he made the Western Union guy stop sending. In the fourth inning of the ball game, I had to stop broadcasting.

"We made a heck of a beef out of that. I wound up in Baseball Commissioner Landis's office in the 333 Building on the following Monday. I'll say this for the judge—he was a tough, rough old boy—but he was conciliatory on this one. He said, 'You've got a very good point; we'll get this straightened out.'"

Toward the end of their noontime visit Harry enjoyed telling Jack about twice having been a guest of Elvis Presley in the 1960s—once at his Graceland home in Memphis after a St. Louis Hawks basketball game and two years later in Las Vegas. Presley initiated the acquaintanceship, introducing himself as "a great Cardinal fan and a Harry Caray fan." They spent hours together on those occasions, with Harry remembering that Presley wanted to talk about "baseball, booze, and broads, and not necessarily in that order."

In March 1994 Brickhouse was invited to record a reminiscence on WGN radio in commemoration of Caray's fiftieth year in broadcasting. At the microphone, Jack spoke extemporaneously:

> I have a story about Harry that really isn't a sports story, even though baseball is involved. It's a story about the great determination and the great courage that this man showed me one time, showed all of us.
> One evening in St. Louis, Harry was crossing the street, and he was hit by a car. What happened was that it broke, I think, every bone in both legs.

He was destined for a lifetime of being crippled; he was destined for a wheelchair—at the best, crutches. Harry Caray lay on his back that entire winter, into the spring, with both legs in a cast every minute; and everybody wondering if he would ever walk again. Harry kept saying, "I will, and I'll be there for opening day."

Well, it just so happened that the Cubs opened the season at St. Louis that year, so I was down there. I was in the Chicago Cubs' dressing room prior to the boys going out on the field, and into that dressing room walked Harry Caray—and I mean walked, briskly. He said, "Told you I'd be here!"

This was a tremendous tribute to the guy's determination, because you know and I know it wouldn't be too tough to become very, very disappointed and melancholy and unhappy about a situation like that. Not only did he walk again, but I'll give you a little tip. Don't take him on in a game of tennis. I made that mistake out in Palm Springs one time a few years later, and the guy ran my legs off.

Harry Caray—demonstrating the determination that it takes to succeed. Happy fiftieth, old friend! I'm glad there are still a few of us left.

CHAPTER 10

Awards and Reflections

"NOTHING IS WORK UNLESS YOU'D RATHER BE DOING something else."
>—George Halas, interviewed
>by Jack Brickhouse, 1975

Those words of George Halas summarize well the Brickhouse career. A high school student during the Great Depression, he was earning money for his family by the age of ten. Yet broadcasting—which he began as a teenager—so suited him that he cannot conceive of a better life. "If I weren't the announcer, I would have been paying my way into those games."

The culmination of his "dream job" came in 1983: the National Baseball Hall of Fame's Ford C. Frick Award—an annual citation initiated in 1978 to honor major-league announcers. For this only child of a young immigrant mother, becoming the seventh recipient of the national award was an emotional experience. He had received other honors—induction into other halls of fame, honorary doctorates, countless civic citations. But the "ultimate honor" was the one from

Cooperstown, New York—a tribute by his colleagues and heroes for a career on behalf of the national pastime.

Selection of Brickhouse as the 1983 recipient was announced in January, with the award presentation in July. "Jack Rosenberg wrote my acceptance speech for me. I wouldn't have changed a comma; it was absolutely perfect."

Rosenberg remembers:

> When he got the call, Jack asked me, "In view of our long association, would you do one more favor—write my speech?" I said, "Of course."
>
> I took some time, and it was a pleasure to do. When I finished, I remember going to Jack's office. "Sit down, and I will read you your speech." It took three minutes flat. "If we go short, you will be the only one in that Hall of Fame ceremony applauded for your brevity. If, however, you start naming those to whom you owe gratitude, you will go on for an hour. For those three minutes, the network stations will carry your entire speech because of its message." When I finished reading it, Jack was crying. I had never seen him cry.

The award was presented at Cooperstown by his Hall of Fame friend Ralph Kiner and by Baseball Commissioner Bowie Kuhn. At the podium Jack gave his speech.

> I stand this day on what I consider the hallowed baseball ground of Cooperstown. I feel at this moment like a man who is sixty feet six inches tall.
>
> On a clear day in this quaint central New York village, you can hear and see and feel the echoes of baseball's storied past. The atmosphere to me is breathless and humbling.

It has been my privilege to broadcast the exploits of the Chicago Cubs and the Chicago White Sox for forty years or more. There in Wrigley Field and Comiskey Park, I have experienced the joy and the heartbreak—probably more of the latter than the former—but Chicago and its beautifully loyal fans have had a resiliency which has kindled a perpetual flame of hope.

In the fantasy of my dreams, I have imagined myself as the announcer for a Cubs–White Sox World Series—a Series that would last seven games, with the final game going extra innings before being suspended because of darkness at Wrigley Field.

Even as I accept this award, my life as a baseball broadcaster flashes before me. The drum beats on. The cities change. The boundaries change. The stadia change. The faces change. The announcers change. But the game remains essentially the same. Nine men on a side, three strikes and you're out. It's a contradiction, baseball is. It can be the simplest of games, yet it can be the most involved. It is the game I love.

The trains, the planes, the cabs, the buses—they have carried me millions of miles through the years to get me where I most wanted to be—the ball game. A reporter once told me that even if *I* didn't make Cooperstown, my suitcase probably would. Fortunately for me, we arrived together.

And I knew I was in the right place almost immediately. I saw a blur. That had to be Brooks Robinson going to his left. I saw a clutch base hit. That had to be George Kell. I saw a majestic high kick on the mound. That had to be Juan Marichal. I saw a quiet, firm image in the dugout. That had to be Walter Alston. I saw a typewriter, or was it a VDT? That had to be Cy Burick. For a boy from Peoria to have his name intertwined with theirs, well . . . only in America.

It is with the deepest sincerity that I thank my company—the WGN Continental Broadcasting Company in Chicago—for believing in the entertainment value of baseball on radio and television—and for believing in me. You will pardon my pride if I insist that our call letters—WGN—are the most respected in the nation. Countless people at WGN and elsewhere have brought me to this broadcasting pinnacle today. You know who you are—and you have my undying gratitude.

Here on this memorable afternoon in Cooperstown, my heart tells me I have traveled the ninety feet from third to home and scored standing up. Thank you very much.

Rosenberg again: "Jack was at his best that day, and he received a standing ovation. When a number of the veteran sportswriters intimated to him that it may have been the finest speech given at the Hall of Fame, he said, 'Why don't you go over and tell Rosey?' I never forgot the fact that he once again remembered me. It was very typical of him."

Even today, Jack singles out as his most exciting baseball event his first major-league broadcast—the White Sox against the Detroit Tigers at Comiskey Park, April 1940. Other highlights include "Willie Mays's catch on Vic Wertz in the 1954 World Series," the Sox clinching the 1959 pennant in Cleveland—and the plane trip home—and in 1970 "Mr. Cub" Ernie Banks's milestone 500th home run.

Yankees manager Casey Stengel talking with Brickhouse and Chicago
reporter Jim Enright and columnist Dave Condon

Chicago Mayor Richard J. Daley in discussion at a Brickhouse testimonial dinner (Photo by Joseph B. Meegan courtesy of the Back of the Yards Neighborhood Council)

Hosting Leo Durocher, the Cubs' Billy Williams, and the Bears' Gale Sayers (Photo by Barney A. Sterling)

With Ernie Banks, 1959 (Photo courtesy of WGN-TV)

"Ernie Banks Day" at Wrigley Field in 1964, with his father, wife, and twin sons (Photo by Barney A. Sterling)

TV prevue

● Free every Sunday with your Chicago Sun-Times

JACK BRICKHOUSE
Broadcasting's Man
of the Year

Chicago Sun-Times' 1968 Broadcasting Man of the Year

A Chicago Bears testimonial for Red Grange: from left, Bill Osmanski, Brickhouse, Grange, Bronko Nagurski, WGN colleague Wally Phillips, Don Hutson, and George Trafton

With George Halas and Bears physician Dr. Ted Fox, 1978

Spring training with pal Jimmy Dykes (Photo by Sam R. Quincey)

"The Tenth Inning" with Sandy Koufax (above) and with Willie Mays
(Photos by Barney A. Sterling)

With Frank Darling, president of the Electrical Workers Union Local 1031, and WGN president Ward Quaal (Photo by Jon's Studio)

Preparing for a WGN broadcast with a player from each season: Chicago Bulls guard Guy Rodgers, White Sox pitcher Gary Peters, and Bears running back Gale Sayers (Photo by Barney A. Sterling)

With Chicago Stadium and Blackhawks owner Arthur Wirtz

Nancy and Ronald Reagan visiting with Brickhouse during the 1976 presidential primary campaign (Photo by Metro News Photos)

With daughter Jeanne and grandson Noah in the early 1980s

In the Cubs' locker room with ageless equipment manager Yosh Kawano

Brickhouse's final home game, 1981 (*Daily Herald* photo, Arlington Heights, Illinois)

The National Baseball
Hall of Fame Veterans
Committee, 1991:
standing: John "Buck"
O'Neil, Billy Herman,
Birdie Tebbetts, Joe L.
Brown, Buzzie Bavasi,
Ernie Harwell, Allen
Lewis, Bob Broeg, Ted
Gabe Paul, Ted
Williams, Brickhouse,
Monte Irvin, Edgar
Munzel, and Bill
Guilfoile of the Hall of
Fame staff; seated:
Stan Musial, Charles
Seeger, Ed Stack, Al
Lopez, and Howard
Talbot Jr. (Photo
courtesy of the National
Baseball Library &
Archive, Cooperstown,
New York)

Promotional picture of Brickhouse trading cards "with a real pro" (Photo courtesy of WGN-TV)

The 1994 reunion of the longtime Cubs broadcasting team of Lou Boudreau, Vince Lloyd, and Jack Brickhouse (Photo courtesy of WGN-TV)

With Harry Caray, 1993

With Gale Sayers at a 1995 fund-raising event (Photo by Barbara Ciurej courtesy of the Foundation for Hearing and Speech Rehabilitation)

With wife, Pat, 1993 (Photo by Stuart-Rodgers Ltd. Photography)

Among his countless interview subjects over the years, one of Jack's most memorable, and one that still troubles him, was a 1960s visit with a years-past baseball star:

Probably the biggest single story in the history of baseball is perhaps also its saddest: the 1919 World Series scandal, in which the Chicago White Sox were accused, and apparently properly so, of throwing the Series to the Cincinnati Reds. This is not to defend the White Sox—but I was told a story that makes me wonder whether justice was completely done.

Some years ago when I was in Bradenton, Florida, covering the Sox spring training, I learned that the Hall of Famer and all-time star Edd Roush was then the clubhouse man for the local ball club. I thought I'd visit with the old boy—he was one of the true greats.

I was pleasantly surprised to find him alone in the clubhouse, so I introduced myself and sat down with him just to talk baseball—reminisce on some great moments of the past.

Somehow the 1919 World Series scandal came into the conversation. Roush was one of the Cincinnati stars, and that year he won the National League batting title. As you know, gamblers approached the White Sox and made their deal, which was later exposed and which caused eight White Sox players to be banned from baseball for life.

Imagine my surprise when Roush said to me, "What a lot of people don't know is that the gamblers approached Cincinnati first, and our guys turned them down." I almost fell out of my chair! After all, the White Sox were not convicted in the court trial. Instead, baseball itself banned them. The new commissioner, Judge Kenesaw Mountain Landis, did it.

One of the White Sox players, Buck Weaver, the great third baseman who had a phenomenal series, was banned along with the others—not because he took money, but because he failed to report it when they approached him. Buck told me personally that was all they had against him—the fact that he didn't report it. In those days baseball was not as strong as it became later. There was no real protection for the players if they got on the wrong side of the gamblers.

My question: Why were the Cincinnati players who were approached by the gamblers not banned for not reporting it? I reported Roush's statement to the office of the commissioner of baseball and even went on the air with the story. I'm still puzzled as to why no one picked up on it. And as I said, justice may not have been complete.

Fifteen years after his official retirement, Jack still maintains an office at WGN-TV. "I retired from the booth in 1981 but not from the business because, as I tell my friends, I have creditors with expensive tastes." He stayed on for three years as a Cubs vice president, saying at the time: "It's a fun thing for me with the pressure off. I'm still a part of it, but if it's a bad game, I can leave in the sixth inning."

On radio, Jack cohosted an evening sports program and for several years presented "Jack Brickhouse's Chicago Cubs Scrapbook" following game broadcasts. He served on selection committees for the college football Heisman Trophy and the National Football Hall of Fame. In 1991 he was appointed to the eighteen-member Baseball Veterans' Hall of Fame Committee, replacing fellow broadcaster Red Barber. The committee chooses players, managers, umpires, and club executives who have been retired from the game for more than fifteen years. Other committee members during Jack's tenure have included Billy Herman, Yogi Berra, Pee Wee Reese, Monte Irvin, Ted Williams, Stan Musial, and White Sox friend Al Lopez. Their selections have included Bill Veeck, Tony Lazzeri, Hal Newhouser, Leo Durocher, Phil Rizzuto, Richie Ashburn, and Mike Schmidt. Jack reports:

> Each year a limited number of guys get voted in. As some get chosen, others move up the list. That's what happened with Durocher and Rizzuto.
>
> Also, mores change. One day the ban on Pete Rose will probably be lifted. Maybe the next generation of Hall officials will claim that he's suffered enough or that his gambling offenses won't seem so horrible—unless it's proven beyond a doubt that he gambled on his own ball club.
>
> As a matter of fact, a visitor not knowing the situation would think that Pete Rose is already in the Hall of Fame. A large Cincinnati Reds display there shows Rose, Johnny Bench, and Joe Morgan in life-size pictures with detailed accounts of their great accomplishments and records.
>
> I was at the Cooperstown ceremony in July 1995, my first trip back since receiving the Frick Award. Richie Ashburn, a veteran inductee, said in his speech: "Our 1962 Mets lost 120 games, a major-

league record. I was the MVP on that team. We lost
our last game of the season at Wrigley Field, when a
Cub triple play in the last inning beat us. Our man-
ager, Casey Stengel, met us at the clubhouse with
'Don't feel bad about it, fellows. It was a team effort.
No *one* man could have pulled that off.' " Ashburn
also stated, "Ron Santo and Nellie Fox belong in the
Hall of Fame." And I agree.

During one evening's entertainment at Cooperstown, Stan Musial, backed up by a big band, gave an
outstanding impromptu harmonica concert. His rendition of "The Wabash Cannonball" brought down
the house.

Jack has been inducted into ten halls of fame, including
the National Sportscasters & Sportswriters Association Hall
of Fame and the American Sportscasters Association Hall of
Fame. In 1986 the man "who broadcast more losing baseball
games than any other man in history" was named the
Chicago Press Veteran of the Year. That award, he said at
the time, "ranks right up there with the Baseball Hall of
Fame. These are your colleagues; you can't fool them. If
they give you a stamp of approval, you ought to be pretty
flattered." The honor also brought Brickhouse his fourth
congratulatory citation in the *Congressional Record*, this
one reported by Illinois representative Henry Hyde.

In 1990, Jack's fiftieth year of broadcasting in Chicago,
he was honored by the City Council. The members approved
a resolution by Alderman Burton Natarus naming a curved
lane along Michigan Avenue, across from the Wrigley Building and near Tribune Tower, "Jack Brickhouse Way." Pat
Brickhouse organized a huge surprise ceremony at the site,

with many wGN and other media colleagues among the invited guests. The event was covered on television and in both the *Tribune* and *Sun-Times*.

Jack has received several honorary doctorates and is probably most proud of the one bestowed in 1990 by his beloved Bradley University in Peoria, where he served as a trustee from 1975 to 1985.

> I built my broadcasting career as a result of marvelous performances by the Bradley basketball teams. But I always felt sensitive that I didn't finish college, so it gave me great pleasure both when I became a trustee and then when I received an honorary Bradley doctorate.
>
> And even though by nature I'm conservative, one of the almost socialistic ideas—if you want to call it that—I embrace is that everyone should be able to get an education. For those who need the money, let the government give it or loan it to them.

In 1994 Jack was named sports rector of the Lincoln Academy of Illinois, an organization established thirty years earlier by Governor Otto Kerner to recognize individuals for achievements that "brought honor to Illinois." In 1968, as an active broadcaster, Jack was awarded the academy's Medal of Lincoln citation.

The following year, 1969, the *Sun-Times* honored him as its "Broadcasting Man of the Year": "His appointment calendar is so jammed it looks like the first draft of a novel. Most of the entries consist of benefits—appearances before various charity and civic organizations for which he accepts no remuneration."

And more than twenty-five years later the description still holds, as Jack volunteers for organizations that include the Boys and Girls Clubs of Chicago, City of Hope, United Cerebral Palsy, the Chicago Baseball Cancer Charities, Cubs Care, and Northwestern Memorial Hospital. "I believe I should give back to the city that's been so good to me." He is active in several charity golf events, especially the Jack Quinlan Memorial Golf Tournament, which he cofounded in tribute to his WGN colleague.

In 1994 Jack became the first recipient of the Israel Sports Humanitarian Award from Shaare Zedek Hospital in Jerusalem. "Having witnessed the damage from sports injuries, when I heard that this hospital was raising funds for a sports medicine department, I knew that I had a cause." He and Pat traveled to Israel to accept the award and help dedicate the facility.

Another invitation he was pleased to accept was narrating "Casey at the Bat" with the Chicago Symphony Orchestra at the 1993 Grant Park Music Festival. The program was described in the *Sun-Times* by its classical-music reviewer:

> Conductor Michael Morgan donned an umpire's vest and the orchestra was divided evenly between Sox caps stage right and Cubs caps stage left.
>
> Looking resplendent in a yellow blazer, brown Hawaiian print shirt and striped, bell-bottomed pants, Brickhouse handled the story of the ill-fated Mudville nine with his customary elan.
>
> For those who wondered how the optimistic announcer would handle such uncharacteristic phrases as "fake," "fraud," and "kill the umpire!" Brickhouse offered an equally elegant reading of sportswriter Grantland Rice's sequel poem, "Casey's Revenge."

Jack was elated: "For a kid from Peoria to wind up appearing before thousands and backed by a world-force orchestra, it was a dream come true."

The broadcaster once described as "hearty, buoyant, and indefatigable" still relishes opportunities for guest appearances in his hometown. "I'm a dues-paying member of the Peoria Baseball Old Timers and have gone down to throw out the first ball of the season at Pete Vonachen Stadium. I say I love Peoria like a mother and Chicago like a wife." While in Peoria, he usually makes a side trip to Grand View Drive, which overlooks rolling wooded hills and the Illinois River valley—which he terms "one of the world's great views." Jack also includes a visit with one of his closest friends, Harold A. "Pete" Vonachen, owner of the Cubs' minor-league team in Peoria. According to Jack, "The Vonachens are probably Peoria's best-known family. Pete has a natural talent for being a good friend, a fun companion, and a good business dealer—all of those things. A great guy."

Throughout his career Jack's upbeat "gee whiz" style of sports broadcasting generated both praise and criticism. *Daily News* columnist Jack Mabley proclaimed in the early 1950s, "There is no better announcer in baseball than Jack Brickhouse," later adding that "baseball announcers are like rutabagas—you either like them or you don't."

Longtime colleague Lindsey Nelson described Jack as "Mr. Sunshine, a most happy fella on the air. It was 'Hey, hey' for the Cubs, and they may be trailing by six in the bottom of the ninth, but 'We're gonna get 'em.' And if we don't get 'em today, we'll get 'em tomorrow. Critics from the print media would take occasional swipes at Brickhouse because he was not more critical of sloppy play when it occurred. The fans didn't seem to want any more criticism, and I certainly didn't want to hear criticism from Brickhouse. He was always such good company, never failing to brighten your day with a story."

On Jack's retirement in 1981, columnist Bob Getz wrote an essay from Wichita, Kansas, that reflected the feelings of many fans:

> I didn't want to believe it. Jack Brickhouse is as much a part of my life and my identity as the schools I went to, the ball park I played at, the neighbors, the teachers, the baseball coaches I had as a kid. . . .
>
> And as the years went by after I left that part of the country, whenever I went back to visit in summer and turned on a ball game, there was Jack Brickhouse, as always. . . .
>
> If Brickhouse had any trademark, it was simply his enthusiasm for the game. As a baseball-crazed kid, you knew he loved the game as much as you did.

And Jack enjoys describing that love of the game:

The enthusiasm was genuine. I always took the position that every major leaguer is one of about 750 of the greatest baseball players in a world of several billion people. In order to reach that position, then, even number 750 has to have certain unique, specialized, exceptional skills, and until he proves otherwise, he's a hero of mine.

The way I look at it, every player on a big-league field in a big-league town was a huge star back in his high school; he was probably the best athlete in the school's history. If he's not the best baseball player in

America today, at least he's made it to the major leagues; he may not make the ballot for the All-Star team, but he's certifiably a big leaguer, and no one will ever be able to take that away from him.

I don't know if kids today still feel such reverence for the concept of the big leagues; expansion really has watered down the meaning of the term, and there are big-league franchises, baseball and otherwise, in cities that never could have hoped to qualify in past decades.

But it means something to me. Maybe this baseball season will pass without my going out to even one game. I'll watch the sportscasts, though, and I'll read the sports pages, and I'll be reminded every day of the summer that this city where I live has been big-league since the idea of big leagues was invented.

Baseball Hall of Fame honoree Jerome Holtzman—heralded by the *Wall Street Journal* as the quintessential baseball writer—has referred to Brickhouse as "my longtime guru" for his knowledge of the sport. Some other Chicagoans, however, criticized him as the irrepressible optimist, the "homer." Writer and Cubs fan Joseph Epstein, who relished many "thrills in Wrigley Field in the fifties," complained:

> Listening to Jack Brickhouse announce a ballgame was like being trapped on a long bus ride with a hardware salesman who believed intensely in his product and knew no jokes. . . . At the end of yet another dreary season, Brickhouse, as chipper as ever (he must have drawn an impressive salary), would find the Cubs "in their familiar role as spoiler." . . . In my more lucid moments I know

that he did not actually bring about all those gray
years of defeat for Chicago teams. But he was
always there at the mike, always cheerful, always
infuriating.

During the years that Jack was the broadcaster for both
Chicago baseball teams, some White Sox fans perceived a
partiality to the Cubs—even though compared with the Sox
the Cubs' records were dismal. Writer Richard Lindberg
made critical remarks about Jack in several Sox histories. But
in his most recent book, *Stealing First in a Two-Team Town*,
Lindberg described the announcer as "a gentle soul and baseball purist" and recognized him for helping secure the final
financial investment that kept the team in Chicago.

In the 1970s syndicated media critic Gary Deeb lam-
pooned Brickhouse as a "Pollyanna house man." Some Deeb
columns, however, generated letter-to-the-editor responses
from the broadcaster's fans—including one from Walter
Schwimmer, who in 1950 produced Jack's pilot golf program
for WGN:

> I am the guy who pioneered bowling for televi-
> sion, golf, bridge. . . . There is hardly a top talent
> who worked in Chicago radio or television who
> did not at one time work for me, from Dave Gar-
> roway to Mike Wallace. That includes Jack Brick-
> house. I will now say categorically that Brickhouse
> is the top sportscaster in the history of Chicago
> radio-TV. . . . If Gary Deeb ever tuned in a Cub
> game that was interrupted by rain and heard Jack
> talk baseball for two hours straight and make it
> sound interesting—he would have to be impressed.

Deeb's complaints became less strident in later years, and
he even good-naturedly confronted his subject at a Brick-

house charity roast: "He's eminently roastable and eminently toastable; I'm glad to be here to do both."

Comfortable with the success he attained, Brickhouse takes criticism in stride. "We all have to develop a thick hide in this business or go look for work as a plumber." Yet he does harbor some regrets, primarily that he has not been recognized for his many broadcasting achievements unrelated to sports. In 1950 *Tribune* columnist Larry Wolters recommended Jack for a George Foster Peabody award, which Wolters described as "the radio and TV equivalent of the Hollywood Oscars." In recognition of a Thanksgiving Day religious program Jack had presented, Wolters wrote, "Nothing radio or television has ever done quite so effectively reflected the universal brotherhood of man. If you missed it, you missed a memorable experience." Through the decades the Peabody Award has remained a coveted goal, as has a lifetime achievement award from Chicago's Museum of Broadcast Communications, which Jack helped found.

Over the years Jack perceived something of a media bias favoring the big-city teams of the East Coast. In that regard he was among those who criticized the 1994 PBS series "Baseball." His description of Mays's famous over-the-shoulder catch is heard within the first minutes of the eighteen-hour program and repeated in a later segment: "Caught by Willie Mays! . . . Willie Mays just brought this crowd to its feet with a catch which must have looked like an optical illusion to a lot of people!" Yet Brickhouse is not identified as the national network broadcaster, nor did the series writers or producers consult him. He felt that many individuals important in the sport went unrecognized, in favor of attention to New York and Boston teams. He *is* pleased that his call of "the catch" is being considered for a new Willie Mays exhibit at the Cooperstown Hall of Fame Museum.

In July of 1994, when the season-ending baseball strike drew near, Jack criticized both the players and the owners:

This sport will probably survive and succeed not because of some of the people involved, but in spite of them. They knew four years ago this would happen; that's when the last contract was signed. Here we are at deadline time, and they haven't figured it out yet.

One of the issues goes back a lot of years. Two straight shooters, who personality-wise were 180 degrees apart, were Phil Wrigley, a laid-back man, and Bill Veeck, a very flamboyant, upfront guy. Both of these men, however, in individual personal conversations with me, made this point in almost the same language: baseball had better do something about the reserve clause, or eventually there will be a problem—maybe a players' union or a problem with Congress. Certainly it has worked out that way.

What I mean about the reserve clause: It was put in by the owners to protect themselves from each other—to prevent the rich owners from buying up all the good players. If that happened, the competition balance would be ruined, and it would be dangerous for the game. So they agreed to put in the reserve clause, which simply meant that if I signed a player, he is now my player. You can't have him unless I trade him, unless I release him, or unless I sell him to you. He cannot negotiate on his own.

As Curt Flood pointed out in the 1970s, this was a form of slavery. I have to say that it's a form of slavery on the elegant side. As the years went by, a players' union was formed, free agency was created—all because baseball, which Wrigley and Veeck both claimed should have been modified, did not modify the reserve clause.

It wasn't until my last few years of broadcasting baseball that the game's owners began to change. For most of my career I was blessed with the opportunity to deal with individuals whose love for the game, in many ways, surpassed their love for the business.

Reflecting on his six-decade broadcasting career, he considers his epitaph: "When someone puts up a tombstone for me, I hope they could write on it, 'Here lies a guy who wasn't a bad reporter.'"

In addition to being a good and versatile reporter, John Beasley "Jack" Brickhouse is an unusual person. With scarcely more than a high school education, he crafted a career through determination, creativity, and intelligence. During the 1950s his popularity as a national sports broadcaster soared. By the 1970s he was the venerable voice of the Chicago Cubs—having bid farewell to six years with the Chicago Bulls and lengthy stints with the White Sox and Bears.

Congenial and cordial, Jack also developed the confidence for confrontations—with a Peoria boss, a university president, a Cubs manager. Adapting the small-town work ethic to the sophisticated big city, he formulated a career that is now a paradigm for nostalgia—the sound of the Big Bands, the popularity of radio, the novelty of television, the joy of baseball—and the virtue of its heroes.

Jack Brickhouse exudes pride in his work and his profession, wistful only that he did not broadcast a Cubs World Series: "Except for the pennant the White Sox won in 1959, baseball championships to me have been mere bubbles in the air, blown away and disintegrated by summer breezes. But then, any team can have a bad century!"

Bibliography

MUCH OF THE MATERIAL FOR THIS BIOGRAPHY OF Jack Brickhouse came from his personal files—primarily correspondence, magazine articles, and newspaper clippings—dating from the early 1930s. Another source was his large audiotape collection of interviews with sports, political, and entertainment personalities.

Throughout his lengthy career Brickhouse was the subject of articles in the sports sections of the *Peoria Journal* and *Star* and all of the Chicago newspapers, especially the *Tribune*. The "Harold Teen" cartoon strips by Carl Ed featuring Jackson Brickhouse and Brick Jackhouse were syndicated by the *Tribune*. During the 1960s Brickhouse wrote a three-times-weekly sports column, "Jack Brickhouse Says," for *Chicago's American*. In 1986 his autobiographical *Thanks for Listening* was published by Diamond Communications, Inc. Other reference sources include:

Books

Alexander, Charles C. *Our Game: An American Baseball History*. New York: Henry Holt, 1991.

Allen, Lee. *100 Years of Baseball*. New York: Bartholomew House, Inc., 1950.

Allen, Maury. *Voices of Sport*. New York: Grosset & Dunlap, 1971.

Allen, Mel, with Ed Fitzgerald. *You Can't Beat the Hours*. New York: Harper & Row, 1964.

Allen, Mel, with Frank Graham, Jr. *It Takes Heart*. New York: Harper & Brothers, 1959.

Anderson, Dave. *Pennant Races: Baseball at Its Best*. New York: Doubleday, 1994.

Aylesworth, Thomas G. *Baseball's Great Dynasties: The Cubs*. New York: Gallery Books, 1990.

Barber, Walter (Red). *The Broadcasters*. New York: Dial Press, 1970.

Barnouw, Erik. *The Golden Web: A History of Broadcasting in the United States, Volume II, 1933 to 1953*. New York: Oxford University Press, 1968.

Berke, Art, and Schmitt, Paul. *This Date in Chicago White Sox History*. Briarcliff Manor, N.Y.: Stein and Day, 1982.

Biles, Roger. *Big City Boss in Depression and War: Mayor Edward J. Kelly of Chicago*. DeKalb: Northern Illinois University Press, 1984.

Blake, Mike. *Baseball Chronicles: An Oral History of Baseball Through the Decades*. Cincinnati: Betterway Books, 1994.

Bosco, Joseph. *The Boys Who Would Be Cubs: A Year in*

the Heart of Baseball's Minor Leagues. New York: William Morrow & Co., 1990.

Boudreau, Lou. *Lou Boudreau: Covering All the Bases*. Champaign, Ill.: Sagamore, 1993.

Brickhouse, Grady G. *The Brickhouse Family History*. Black Hawk, S.D.: G. G. Brickhouse, 1987.

Brickhouse, Jack. *Jack Brickhouse's Major League Record Book*. Chicago: WGN, 1950–1971.

———. *Thanks for Listening!* South Bend, IN: Diamond Communications, 1986.

Broadwater, Jeff. *Adlai Stevenson and American Politics*. New York: Twayne Publishers, 1994.

Brown, Warren. *The Chicago Cubs*. New York: G. P. Putnam's Sons, 1946.

———. *The Chicago White Sox*. New York: G. P. Putnam's Sons, 1952.

Caray, Harry, with Bob Verdi. *Holy Cow!* New York: Villard Books, 1989.

Chadwick, Bruce. *The Chicago Cubs: Memories and Memorabilia of the Wrigley Wonders*. New York: Abbeville, 1994.

———. *The Chicago Cubs Trivia Book*. New York: St. Martin's Press, 1994.

Cohen, Richard M., and Neft, David S. *The World Series*. New York: Macmillan, 1986.

Condon, Dave. *The Go-Go Chicago White Sox*. New York: Coward-McCann, 1960.

Creamer, Robert W. *Babe: The Legend Comes to Life*. New York: Simon and Schuster, 1974.

———. *Baseball in '41*. New York: Viking, 1991.

Dickey, Glenn. *The History of the World Series Since 1903*. New York: Stein and Day, 1984.

Durocher, Leo. *Nice Guys Finish Last*. New York: Simon and Schuster, 1975.

Dykes, Jimmie, and Dexter, Charles O. *You Can't Steal First Base*. Philadelphia: J. B. Lippincott, 1967.

Edwards, Bob. *Fridays with Red: A Radio Friendship*. New York: Simon & Schuster, 1993.

Enright, Jim. *Baseball's Great Teams: Chicago Cubs*. New York: Collier Books, 1975.

———. *March Madness: The Story of High School Basketball in Illinois*. Bloomington: Illinois High School Assn., 1977.

Eskenazi, Gerald. *Bill Veeck: A Baseball Legend*. New York: McGraw-Hill, 1988.

Feinstein, John. *Play Ball*. New York: Villard, 1993.

Fink, John. *WGN: A Pictorial History*. Chicago: WGN, Inc., 1961.

Frisch, Frank. *Frank Frisch: The Fordham Flash*. Garden City, N.Y.: Doubleday, 1962.

Frommer, Harvey. *Baseball's Greatest Managers*. New York: Franklin Wats, 1985.

Fulk, David, and Riley, Dan, eds. *The Cubs Reader*. Boston: Houghton Mifflin, 1991.

Gifford, Barry. *The Neighborhood of Baseball: A Personal History of the Chicago Cubs*. New York: E. P. Dutton, 1981.

Gold, Eddie. *Eddie Gold's White Sox and Cubs Trivia Book*. Chicago: Follett, 1981.

Gold, Eddie, and Ahrens, Art. *The New Era Cubs, 1941–1985*. Chicago: Bonus Books, 1985.

Gowdy, Curt, with Al Hirshberg. *Cowboy at the Mike*. Garden City, N.Y.: Doubleday, 1966.

Gowdy, Curt, with John Powers. *Seasons to Remember: The*

Way It Was in American Sports, 1945–1960. New York: HarperCollins, 1993.

Graham, Frank. *The New York Giants: An Informal History.* New York: G. P. Putnam's Sons, 1952.

Halas, George, with Gwen Morgan and Arthur Veysey. *Halas by Halas: The Autobiography of George Halas.* New York: McGraw-Hill, 1979.

Halberstam, David. *October, 1964.* New York: Villard Books, 1994.

———. *Summer of '49.* New York: William Morrow, 1989.

Harwell, Ernie. *Baseball Is Their Business.* New York: Random House, 1952.

———. *Tuned to Baseball.* South Bend, Ind.: Diamond Communications, 1985.

Heise, Kenan, and Baumann, Ed. *Chicago Originals.* Chicago: Bonus Books, 1990.

Heise, Kenan, and Frazel, Mark. *Hands on Chicago.* Chicago: Bonus Books, 1987.

Helyar, John. *Lords of the Realm: The Real History of Baseball.* New York: Villard, 1994.

Holtzman, Jerome, ed. *No Cheering in the Press Box.* New York: Holt, 1974.

Honig, Donald. *Baseball America: The Heroes of the Game and the Times of Their Glory.* New York: Macmillan, 1985.

Hynd, Noel. *The Giants of the Polo Grounds.* New York: Doubleday, 1988.

Kelley, Brent. *Baseball Stars of the 1950s.* Jefferson, N.C.: McFarland, 1993.

Kilian, Michael, Fletcher, Connie, and Ciccone, F. Richard. *Who Runs Chicago?* New York: St. Martin's Press, 1979.

Klein, Jerry. *Peoria!* Peoria, Ill.: Visual Communications, 1985.

Kupcinet, Irving. *Kup's Chicago.* Cleveland: World Pub. Co., 1962.

Kupcinet, Irving, with Paul Neimark. *Kup: A Man, an Era, a City.* Chicago: Bonus Books, 1988.

Langford, Jim. *The Game Is Never Over: An Appreciative History of the Chicago Cubs.* South Bend, Ind.: Icarus Press, 1982.

Lansche, Jerry. *Stan the Man Musial: Born to Be a Ballplayer.* Dallas, Texas: Taylor Publishing Co., 1994.

Lenburg, Jeff. *Baseball's All-Star Game: A Game-by-Game Guide.* Jefferson, N.C.: McFarland, 1986.

Leu, Bob, with Henry Jacobs. *Good Evening, Bradley Basketball Fans.* Peoria, Ill.: Walfred Co., 1976.

Lewis, Tom. *Empire of the Air: The Men Who Made Radio.* New York: HarperCollins, 1991.

Lieb, Fred. *Baseball As I Have Known It.* New York: Grosset & Dunlap, 1977.

Lindberg, Richard. *Stealing First in a Two-Team Town.* Champaign, Ill.: Sagamore, 1994.

———. *Stuck on the Sox.* Evanston: Sassafras Press, 1978.

———. *Who's on 3rd?: The Chicago White Sox Story.* South Bend, Ind.: Icarus Press, 1983.

Logan, Bob. *The Bulls and Chicago: A Stormy Affair.* Chicago: Follett, 1975.

Mantle, Mickey, with Mickey Herskowitz. *All My Octobers: My Memories of Twelve World Series When the Yankees Ruled Baseball.* New York: HarperCollins, 1994.

Michael, Paul. *Professional Football's Greatest Games.* Englewood Cliffs, N.J.: Prentice-Hall, 1972.

Minoso, Orestes, with Herb Fagen. *Just Call Me Minnie: My*

Six Decades in Baseball. Champaign, Ill.: Sagamore, 1994.

Moore, Joseph Thomas. *Pride Against Prejudice: The Biography of Larry Doby.* New York: Greenwood Press, 1988.

Nathan, David H. *Baseball Quotations.* Jefferson, N.C.: McFarland & Co., 1991.

Nelson, Lindsey. *Hello, Everybody, I'm Lindsey Nelson.* New York: Morrow, 1985.

Nemec, David. *The Great American Baseball Team Book.* New York: Plume, 1992.

Oakley, J. Ronald. *Baseball's Last Golden Age, 1946–1960.* Jefferson, N.C.: McFarland & Co., 1994.

Okkonen, Marc. *Baseball Memories, 1950–1959.* New York: Sterling, 1993.

Peary, Danny, ed. *We Played the Game: 65 Players Remember Baseball's Greatest Era, 1947–1964.* New York: Hyperion, 1994.

Phalen, Rick. *Our Chicago Cubs: Inside the History and the Mystery of Baseball's Favorite Franchise.* South Bend, Ind.: Diamond Communications, 1992.

Pierson, Robert L. *Riots Chicago Style.* Great Neck, N.Y.: Todd & Honeywell, 1984.

Pope, Edwin. *Baseball's Greatest Managers.* Garden City, N.Y.: Doubleday, 1960.

Rader, Benjamin G. *Baseball: A History of America's Game.* Urbana: University of Illinois Press, 1992.

————. *In Its Own Image: How Television Has Transformed Sports.* New York: The Free Press, 1984.

Reichler, Joseph L., ed. *The Baseball Encyclopedia: The Complete and Official Record of Major League Baseball.* New York: Macmillan, 1988.

Reichler, Joseph L. *Baseball's Great Moments*. New York: Crown, 1979.

Reinsch, J. Leonard. *Getting Elected: From Radio and Roosevelt to Television and Reagan*. New York: Hippocrene Books, 1988.

Rizzuto, Phil, with Tom Horton. *The October Twelve: Five Years of New York Yankee Glory, 1949–1953*. New York: Tom Doherty Associates, 1994.

Rollow, Cooper. *Cooper Rollow's Bears Football Book*. Ottawa, Ill.: Jameson Books, 1985.

Scheinin, Richard. *Field of Screams: The Dark Underside of America's National Pastime*. New York: W. W. Norton, 1994.

Smelser, Marshall. *The Life that Ruth Built: A Biography*. New York: Quadrangle, 1975.

Smith, Curt. *The Storytellers, From Mel Allen to Bob Costas: Sixty Years of Baseball Tales from the Broadcast Booth*. New York: Macmillan, 1995.

———. *Voices of the Game*, rev. ed. New York: Simon & Schuster, 1992.

Smith, Myron J. Jr., comp. *Baseball: A Comprehensive Bibliography*. Jefferson, N.C.: McFarland, 1986; rev. ed., 1993.

Smith, Robert. *World Series: The Games and the Players*. Garden City, N.Y.: Doubleday, 1967.

Stein, Irving M. *The Ginger Kid: The Buck Weaver Story*. Albuquerque, N.M.: Brown & Benchmark, 1992.

Talley, Rick. *The Cubs of '69: Reflections of the Team That Should Have Been*. Chicago: Contemporary Books, 1989.

Vanderberg, Bob. *Sox: From Lane and Fain to Zisk and Fisk*. Chicago: Chicago Review Press, 1982.

Vass, George. *George Halas and the Chicago Bears*. Chicago: Henry Regnery, 1971.

Vecchione, Joseph J., ed. *The New York Times Book of Sports Legends*. New York: Random House, 1991.

Veeck, Bill, with Ed Linn. *The Hustler's Handbook*. New York: G. P. Putnam's Sons, 1965.

———. *Veeck—As in Wreck*. New York: New American Library, 1986.

Voight, David Q. *America Through Baseball*. Chicago: Nelson-Hall, 1976.

Walker, Leo. *The Wonderful Era of the Great Dance Bands*. Berkeley, Ca.: Howell-North Books, 1964.

Watters, Mary. *Illinois in the Second World War*. 2 vols. Springfield: Illinois State Historical Library, 1951–52.

Whittingham, Richard. *Bears, in Their Own Words*. Chicago: Contemporary Books, 1991.

———. *The Chicago Bears: An Illustrated History*. Chicago: Rand McNally, 1979.

Wilber, Cynthia J. *For the Love of the Game: Baseball Memories from the Men Who Were There*. New York: William Morrow, 1992.

Will, George F. *Men at Work: The Craft of Baseball*. New York: Macmillan, 1990.

Williams, Billy, and Haag, Irv. *Billy: The Classic Hitter*. Chicago: Rand McNally, 1974.

Yates, Louis A. R. *A Proud Heritage: Bradley's History, 1897–1972*. Peoria, Ill.: Bradley University, 1974.

Young, Linda. *Hail to the Orange and Blue! 100 Years of Illinois Football Tradition*. Champaign, Ill.: Sagamore, 1990.

Zimmerman, Paul D., and Schaap, Dick. *The Year the Mets Lost Last Place*. New York: World Publishing, 1969.

NEWSPAPERS

Chicago's American, Chicago Daily News, Chicago Sun, Chicago Sun-Times, Chicago Tribune: 1940–1995.
Peoria Journal, Peoria Star, Peoria Journal-Star: 1934–1995.

Other titles and issues with pertinent information include:

Albany (N.Y.) Times-Union, December 12, 1954
Arlington Heights (Ill.) Daily Herald, June 24, 1981; October 19, 1983
Avon Sentinel, August 3, 1950
Canton Daily Ledger, March 23, 1938
Chicago Merchandise Mart Reporter, January 15, 1948
Chicago River Clipper, February, 1982
Chicago Today, May 18, 1969
LaSalle-Peru-Oglesby (Ill.) Daily Post-Tribune, February 27, 1946
Milwaukee (Wis.) Journal, August 18, 1981
New York Post, August 11, 1952
Newton (Iowa) Daily News, June 17, 1952
Phoenix Arizona Republic, March 31, 1982
Racine (Wis.) Journal-Times, August 20, 1978
St. Petersburg (Fla.) Times, March 12, 1952
Wichita (Kans.) Eagle-Beacon, October 7, 1981
Wilmette (Ill.) Life, July 8, 1971

PERIODICALS

Baseball Digest, August 1948, December 1957, June 1959, July 1964, August 1965, March 1990

Baseball Magazine, December 1951, November 1952, November and December 1953

Billboard, July 29, 1944

Chicago, May 1980, March 1994

Chicago Cubs *Vine Line*, August 1986

Chicago History, vol. 4 (1975), 5 (1976–77), March 1993

Chicago Times, March/April 1988

Congressional Record (Washington, D.C.), September 26, 1986

Hiram Walker Spirit, June 1944

Jerusalem Post Magazine, October 21, 1994

Look, January 16, 1951

Radio and Television Mirror, June 1948

Radio Mirror Magazine, March 1949

The Sporting News, March 1, 1950; July 4 and October 3, 1951; May 25, 1955; June 26, 1957

Sports Illustrated, September 13, 1971

Variety, July 26, 1944; September 5, 1945; March 7, 1951; May 26 and October 6, 1954

MISCELLANEOUS

Printed programs, schedules, yearbooks
Otto Kerner 1973 trial transcript
WGN, WMBD press releases

In addition to the preceding sources, the audio- and video-
tape collections at the Chicago Museum of Broadcast Communications provided significant material both by and about
Jack Brickhouse.

Index

221